Sexting and Revenge Pornography

T0386217

This book considers the rapidly evolving, both legally and socially, nature of image-based abuse for both minors and adults. Drawing mainly from UK data, legislation and case studies, the book presents a thesis that the law is, at best, struggling to keep up with some fundamental issues around image-based abuse, such as the sexual nature of the crimes and the long-term impact on victims, and at worst, in the case of supporting minors, it is not fit for purpose. It shows, through empirical and legislative analysis, that the dearth of education around this topic, coupled with cultural norms, creates a victim-blaming culture that extends into adulthood. It proposes both legislative developments and the need for wider stakeholder engagement to understand and support victims, and the impact the non-consensual sharing of intimate images can have on their long-term mental health and life in general. The book is of interest to scholars of law, criminology, sociology, police and socio-technical studies, and also to those who practice law, law enforcement or have a wider social care role in both child and adult safeguarding.

Andy Phippen is Professor of Digital Rights at Bournemouth University

Maggie Brennan is a Lecturer in Forensic Psychology at the University of Plymouth

Sexting and Revenge Pornography

Legislative and Social Dimensions of a Modern Digital Phenomenon

Andy Phippen and Maggie Brennan

LONDON AND NEW YORK

First published 2021
by Routledge
2 Park Square, Milton Park, Abingdon, Oxon OX14 4RN

and by Routledge
52 Vanderbilt Avenue, New York, NY 10017

Routledge is an imprint of the Taylor & Francis Group, an informa business

© 2021 Andy Phippen and Maggie Brennan

The right of Andy Phippen and Maggie Brennan to be identified as authors of this work has been asserted by them in accordance with sections 77 and 78 of the Copyright, Designs and Patents Act 1988.

Trademark notice: Product or corporate names may be trademarks or registered trademarks, and are used only for identification and explanation without intent to infringe.

British Library Cataloguing-in-Publication Data
A catalogue record for this book is available from the British Library

Library of Congress Cataloging-in-Publication Data
A catalog record has been requested for this book

ISBN: 978-1-138-55577-8 (hbk)
ISBN: 978-1-315-14969-1 (ebk)

Typeset in Galliard
by Deanta Global Publishing Services, Chennai, India

Contents

Foreword

Since its establishment in 2015, the Revenge Porn Helpline has helped thousands of victims to recover from the impact of the non-consensual sharing of images and other media, providing emotional support so that victims realise they are not on their own and giving legal and practical advice. We help with the takedown of illegally posted material and have good working relationships with many in the internet industry. We can provide legal advice and referral to the police who will pursue abusers and bring them to justice.

Revenge pornography or the more correct terms of non-consensual sharing of intimate images or image-based abuse can have a devastating and long-term impact on a victim's life. There is no "typical" victim of image-based abuse, they come from all genders, sexualities and social classes. But one thing that is common to a lot of the victims we speak to is that they are at the end of their tether before they ask for help. They feel they have nowhere else to turn, and do not know what else to do. They often feel alone and unsupported, and one of the first things we do is make them realise they do not have to deal with things on their own, and that the law is on their side.

Since the introduction of "revenge pornography legislation" – section 33 of the Criminal Justice and Courts Act 2015 in England and Wales, and The Abusive Behaviour and Sexual Harm Act 2016 in Scotland – there has, at least, been legislation that can be consistently applied to support victims of image-based abuse. However, while this is a step in the right direction, we cannot assume that because the law exists, image-based abuse will no longer be a problem. In this book, the authors discuss threat, anonymity of victims and consistency of support from law enforcement. We are glad to have been able to provide them with access to both staff and our cases, and they have explored the variety of abuse, impact upon victims, challenges they face in gaining support from those one might hope would aid them and how we might develop a more holistic approach to helping them. They have done an excellent job of distilling the broad range of cases we deal with to focus on the salient points of positive change with the legislation, and the challenges victims still have in the criminal justice system and, more widely, society in general in terms of lack of support and judgemental reactions to their abuse.

While the relationship between revenge pornography and teen sexting might at first seem to be strange bedfellows, we very much agree that these acts, and the associated legislation and educative approaches, should be considered within the same analysis. The Revenge Porn Helpline supports adult victims of image-based abuse, as this is what the legislation defines. However, we see from adults the same messages given to young people in schools – victims believe it's their fault the images or media were shared because "I shouldn't have taken the image in the first place" or "once it's online there's nothing I can do about it". We can see that the approach taken in tackling teen sexting has an impact on adult victims, and we share the concerns regarding the application of legislation developed to protect young people now being used to threaten or even prosecute them. And we see attitudes of adult abusers being shaped in their formative experiences – the non-consensual sharing of images must be seen as wrong at any age, and the focus of blame should be with the sharer, not the taker of the image. We need to see a continuum of support for victims, from youth into adulthood: it seems curious we can support an 18-year-old victim of image-based abuse but a 17-year-old experiencing similar will have to be told they have broken the law.

While the legislation to support adult victims of image-based abuse is a massive step forward for those of us involved in adult online safeguarding, there is still much to do. As this book points out, one fundamental aspect of this is the legislative support for minors who become victims of image-based abuse. We also need to see an education curriculum that moves away from "it's illegal, you shouldn't do it" to focus on the non-consensual sharing of images and the actions of the abuse, and to move society away from a victim-blaming culture. If someone wishes to take and share intimate images, consensually, with a partner, it is not their fault if the partner then chooses to betray consent and trust and share it further. The sharing of images is a part of many relationships, and the focus of blame should lie with the abuser who chooses to send them to others. We need consistency of legislation that supports victims of all ages and focuses punishment on those who have chosen, maliciously, to non-consensually share images and media, rather than punish those who are already suffering.

This book makes a compelling case for both changes in law and culture using a strong evidence base and legislative analysis. This is a text for anyone involved in online safeguarding, and we are delighted to have had the opportunity to work with the authors on this important work.

Sophie Mortimer, Revenge Porn Helpline
Manager, May 2020

1 Call It What It Is – Image-Based Abuse

This book focuses primarily on the non-consensual sharing of intimate images and videos or image-based abuse – perhaps better known as sexting and revenge pornography – as well as the challenge society faces in supporting victims, the complexities in legislation, the difference between legislative responses and grass-root behaviours and an analysis of how we can actually move forwards in our thinking, policy and legislation in this area. Ultimately, this book will contribute to getting to a place where victims are supported, potential abusers are deterred, abusers are punished and held accountable and stakeholders in this space are informed about how to tackle the social challenges presented by the non-consensual sharing of intimate images among both minors and adults.

In order to address these two social phenomena, the majority of legislative and policy discussion resides within the UK. This is primarily due to the fact that all authors have actively researched or practised in this jurisdiction and that is where the empirical evidence base for this work lies. However, throughout the book, examples of other jurisdictions will also be brought in to illustrate similarities and differences in legislation and policy approaches – the legislative and practice challenges faced as a result of the non-consensual sharing of intimate images are certainly not constrained to the UK. We should also stress, as with any text that explores legislation and practice in a fast-moving field, the evidence and analysis presented are accurate at the time of writing. However, one cannot predict policy changes that might affect this field, and while, where possible, issues as presented in a generic way using the current state of things as a lens with which to consider the nature of image-based abuse and how society responds to it.

One of the fundamental tenets of this book is that policy needs to evolve from evidence, and without a good understanding of the context, legislation will always fall short. We risk falling back into legislative hyperactivity,[1] which was so strongly criticised as being endemic in the last UK Labour government, where legislation was thrown at any social ill because it was easier than addressing the

---

1 Stevenson, K., & Harris, C. (2008). "Inaccessible and unknowable: Accretion and uncertainty in modern criminal law". *Liverpool Law Review*, 29(3), 247–267.

broader stakeholder engagement to tackle the problem, which in the main failed to tackle the issues it aimed to legislate against. Is legislation intended as a means to promote ethical and moral practice, or to punish those who wish to act in an immoral manner? If one does not understand the complexity of the social context in which issues such as sexting and revenge pornography exist, legislation will always fail on both counts.

In this book, the social contexts of both sexting and revenge pornography are explored, before considering the legislation currently available to protect victims and punish abusers. Once these two aspects have been established, the third part of the book will consider where and why legislation is failing, how it needs to be updated and what are the broader policy areas that need to be tackled in a more pragmatic manner such that all stakeholders in online safeguarding are brought to bear in tackling these issues. Throughout the book, considerable empirical evidence will be drawn upon from the work of some of the authors – from surveys, qualitative discussions, workshops and ethnographic experiences with victims, as well as potential victims and abusers, and others who are stakeholders in this space. As a result of presenting a robust evidence base one would hope the policy direction can move forwards in this area because it has stagnated for many years, arguably as a result of focusing on the act, rather than wider social aspects of image-based abuse among both minors and adults. While the generation and distribution of an intimate image or video are central to both sexting and revenge pornography, prevention, victim support and appropriate punishment for abusers should look far more broadly. One of the authors of this book began working with young people around the then-emerging "sexting" phenomenon in 2008. After ten years working with young people around sexting, one thing is very clear – attitudes towards sexting by young people have changed little in this time. More specifically:

1. You shouldn't do it, because it's illegal
2. If you self-generate and send an image, it's your fault if it distributed without your consent
3. Once it's out there, there is nothing you can do
4. The victim deserves the abuse they receive if an image or video of them gets shared further

During this ten-year period, there has been much policy debate around teen sexting and how it might be prevented, there have been many resources developed for education and many young people have sat through many assemblies and classes in schools giving them clear messages around reasons not to self-generate and send intimate images, yet they still do it, and they still have the same attitudes about it. Something is clearly failing.

In order to understand what is failing, it is worthwhile taking a step back and reflecting on more fundamental issues affecting this policy space. This provides a useful starting point for discussion and one that will be returned to many times throughout this book.

It is acknowledged that the context of sexting and revenge pornography is based in the broader domain of "online safety" – the theory and practice of ensuring that citizens can engage with online technology and services safely without fear of abuse, threat or harm. Work in this field is well established in both policy and practice and has been thoroughly reviewed elsewhere (for example, in[2]). However, there are a number of aspects that we can draw from this work that are useful starting points to exploring sexting and revenge pornography. Drawing upon previous work, and also a collective expertise of over 40 years working as academics, legal and educational practitioners in the field, several key observations can be drawn from the broader online safety space which is shared within the problem domain of this book:

1. Policy directions will generally focus upon prohibitive approaches because they are politically the least contentious (although arguably also the least successful)
2. Just because technology facilitated an issue, it doesn't mean technology will prevent social problems from occurring (although it can help)
3. In a vacuum of evidence, opinions become an adequate substitute for facts
4. Everyone uses digital technology; therefore, everyone has an opinion on how it might best be "made safe"
5. Statutory pressure can sometimes result in a "do something" attitude

Policy frequently drives practice in this field, yet it still is, of itself, reactive to social behaviours. While one of the authors has been researching in the field of online safety since 2006, exploring, in particular, young people's use of technology and how it impacts on their lives, policy response can take longer. Arguably, the UK only saw clear statutory guidance around "online safety" in schools in September 2016, when the government published its "Keeping Children Safe in Education" statutory guidance for schools and colleges on safeguarding children and safer recruitment.[3] Within it, for the first time, it was made clear that schools had responsibilities to ensure children were protected from risks associated with online technology, that school governors were responsible for ensuring that such practice took place and that staff were up to date in their knowledge in the area. In addition, it listed a collection of resources that were "not exhaustive but should provide a useful starting point" – the starting point being links to typical websites that provided information and resources around online safety.

2 Phippen, A. (2016). "Children's online behaviour and safety: Policy and rights challenges". Springer.
3 UK Government (2019). "Keeping Children Safe in Education 2019 Update". https://as sets.publishing.service.gov.uk/government/uploads/system/uploads/attachment_data/file /835733/Keeping_children_safe_in_education_2019.pdf

Policy in this particular area highlights a number of key issues related to the role of legislation in controlling access to content or managing online social behaviours:

1. "Do something, anything!!"
2. Implement legislation that might not be possible with the technology available
3. Rapidly implement legislation without understanding the broader social context
4. Use older legislation to tackle something for which it was never intended
5. Legislation has knock-on effects that impact on the rights of those wishing to engage in legal behaviour online
6. The legislation fails to achieve what it set out to do

Or, to put it another way – the Politician's Syllogism:[4]

"We need to do something"
"This is something"
"Let's do this!"

This knee jerk policy approach has existed for a quite a while and has been identified in many times in geek culture. The "Four Horsemen of the Infocalypse" is a term coined by Timothy C May[5] to reflect the typical policy response to any technological innovation a government might wish to control or to win over public opinion to back tougher regulation – claim the technology is used by one or more of the Four Horsemen Infocalypse – terrorists, paedophiles, drug dealers and money launderers – and one can win the public over. While May introduced this concept related to controlling the use of encryption by the public (the ripples of this can still be seen to this day, for example, with Amber Rudd's claim that "ordinary people" don't need to use encryption in 2017[6] and the UK Government's recent unease at Facebook's proposed use of end-to-end encryption in its Messenger platform[7]), this has been applied to many technological

4 Chen (2007). "The politician's fallacy and the Politician's Apology". https://devblogs.mic rosoft.com/oldnewthing/20070226-01/?p=27853
5 May (1994). "Crypto Anarchy and Virtual Communities". http://groups.csail.mit.edu/ma c/classes/6.805/articles/crypto/cypherpunks/may-virtual-comm.html
6 Burgess, M. (2017). "The 'real People' Using Encryption for Privacy Protection". https:// www.wired.co.uk/article/uk-encryption-whatsapp-amber-rudd
7 UK Government (2019). "Open Letter to Mark Zuckerberg". https://assets.publishing.serv ice.gov.uk/government/uploads/system/uploads/attachment_data/file/836569/Open_le tter_from_the_Home_Secretary_-_alongside_US_Attorney_General_Barr__Secretary_of_ Homeland_Security__Acting__McAleenan__and_Australian_Minister_for_Home_Affairs_D utton_-_to_Mark_Zuckerberg.pdf

innovations, such as Tor, WhatsApp, Bitcoin, peer-to-peer file sharing and social media in general. The general approach is similar every time:

1. Identify a target that you wish to control or legislate
2. Identify a common fear most people will have that is difficult to defend against, such as one of the Four Horsemen
3. Use the media to show that the target is used by these groups (while ignoring many more prevalent positive uses of the target)
4. Claim that banning or controlling the target is the only way to prevent the bad guys using it, and if you're opposed to that, the bad guys win

The Policy of Image-Based Abuse

In this book, the social context of teen sexting and adult revenge pornography is explored and makes a contribution to the policy debate around how society might "stop" these practices, alongside arguments around how a focus on practice rather than root causes might ultimately fail to address the social changes these issues cause. Although ultimately, society must face the honest truth that these practices cannot be stopped, in the same way that other "antisocial"[8] practices such as drug-taking and the excessive consumption of alcohol cannot be stopped. At best, a government can put legislative measures in place to protect both society as a whole and also the victims of abuse arising from these acts. Any policy that starts from the viewpoint that we will stop this is doomed to fail.

There is no doubt that both teen sexting and the broad adult context of revenge pornography, acts that utilise digital technology to distribute intimate images or videos, can be problematic and cause serious negative impacts on victims as a result of repercussive damage such as breaches of privacy, abuse, harassment, shame, coercion or exploitation that might arise from such acts. This is why terms such as *image-based abuse* and the *non-consensual sharing of intimate images* are more useful. It is rarely the act of self-generating (an equally problematic term that will be returned to later in this text) an image or video that itself causes harm. It is the further sharing of the image or possession of the image by abusers that result in victimisation and abuse. Yet policy remains focused on the act itself.

Sexting and Revenge Pornography – Modern Phenomena

This text will explore how legislation, and associated policy discussions, have attempted to tackle these social issues. It will explore how legislation is used as both a means to change behaviour through the threat of punishment and where

---

8 The quotations are deliberate – much exchange of intimate imagery is a normal part of a 21st-century relationship. The antisocial element stems from those wishing to abuse as a result of being in possession of said images.

legislation can be used to help and support victims. However, to continue the theme established in this introduction, it will show that with a failure to understand the context in detail, a lack of understanding of the complex social setting within which these acts takes place, one can only ever hope to have superficial impact upon the problems being tackled. Through the use of empirical evidence, this research will also show how poorly thought out legislation can be severely lacking in the protection of victims and, particularly in the case of teen sexting, can actually exacerbate the harm to the victim, rather than aid them.

Given that the catalyst act within teen sexting and revenge pornography is the same – the "self-generation" of an intimate image or video that is distributed to one or more recipients – one might question why these two social phenomena, while similar in practice, are addressed distinctly. One might also argue that the terms are interchangeable – adult "sexting" can result in revenge pornography, as such minors carrying out the same acts.

There is little equivalent definition in law for "sexting" because the legislation used to regulate behaviour around this phenomenon achieved ascent far prior to the term reaching public conciousness. If one considers one of the most widely used definitions of sexting for the purposes of this book, from the National Society for the Prevention of Cruelty to Children (NSPCC)[9] in the UK:

Sexting or sending nudes is when someone shares a sexual message, naked or semi-naked image, video or text message with another person. It doesn't have to be a nude image of them and could be an image of someone else.

A definition of revenge pornography frequently used from Citron and Franks' work:[10]

The distribution of sexually explicit images of an individual without their consent.

Or, to draw from the legislation itself:[11]

Disclosing Private Sexual Images with Intent to Cause Distress.

There is clearly an overlap between the definitions – self-produced intimate images that are, in general, "voluntarily" shared. However, the perception that images are generated voluntarily should be challenged strongly. While the creator of the image will usually also be the initial distributor of the image, whether or not the image is

---

9 NSPCC (n.d.). "Sexting and Sending Nudes". https://www.nspcc.org.uk/preventing-abus e/keeping-children-safe/sexting/
10 Citron, D., and Franks, M. (2014). "Criminalizing revenge porn". *Wake Forest Law Review*, *49*, 345–391.
11 UK Government (2015). "Section 33, Criminal Justice and Courts Act 2015". http://www .legislation.gov.uk/ukpga/2015/2/section/33/enacted

shared under the generator's own free will depends on the specific context. One thing from a lot of the case study work presented throughout this text will show that while one might "volunteer" an image and have it sent from one's own device, the image may be as a result of pressure, coercion or extortion. The notion of the self-generated, "volunteered" image as a central point of focus in legislative development is one that fails to acknowledge the broader context in which the original sharing might take place, and that this, of itself, might be an abusive act. This is something that will be returned to in far more detail later in this book.

There is also a distinction in agency between these two acts that is equally problematic when, in reality, the abuse or harm to the victim will generally emerge from the non-consensual sharing and resultant image-based abuse – with "teen sexting", the focus is on the initial act of self-generating and sending an image or video. With revenge pornography, the definition focuses on the non-consensual sharing of an image or video. This is reflected in the legislation, and its enforcement, discussed in more detailed throughout this book and related to the commonly held social understanding of the terms – sexting is a youth practice, revenge pornography is related to adult behaviour. Therefore, policy, education and prevention through the enforcement of the law for sexting lies in prohibition – *let's stop children doing this* – whereas when the "self-generator" is an adult, the focus lies in the punishment of those who distributed the media in a non-consensual manner.

Moreover, the public discourse around the phenomena also differs. A brief analysis on Google Trends will show that while "sexting" emerged into public consciousness in 2008, "revenge pornography" didn't really arise as a phenomenon until 2012 (Figures 1.1 and 1.2).

While Google Trend data only gives an indication of a term's popularity over a given time (in our cases since Google began), and therefore, isn't an accurate measure on the volume of search over time, it can show the relative popularity across the years, and it is clear to see that sexting is a more generalised term that has existed in the public psyche for longer than revenge pornography.

More specifically, and one of the driving forces behind the distinction, the legislation is also distinct. Legislation around teen sexting is very different to revenge pornography.

While the legislative perspective is explored in far more depth in Chapters 4 and 5, it is worth reviewing this when exploring the foundations of revenge pornography and teen sexting.

For teen (and pre-teen) sexting, the UK legislation related is:

* S1 1978 Protection of Children Act[12]
* S45 2003 Sexual Offences Act[13] (extending PCA offence to under 18s)

---

12 UK Government (1978). "Protection of Children Act 1978". http://www.legislation.go v.uk/ukpga/1978/37
13 UK Government (2003). "Section 45, Sexual Offences Act 2003". http://www.legislati on.gov.uk/ukpga/2003/42/section/45

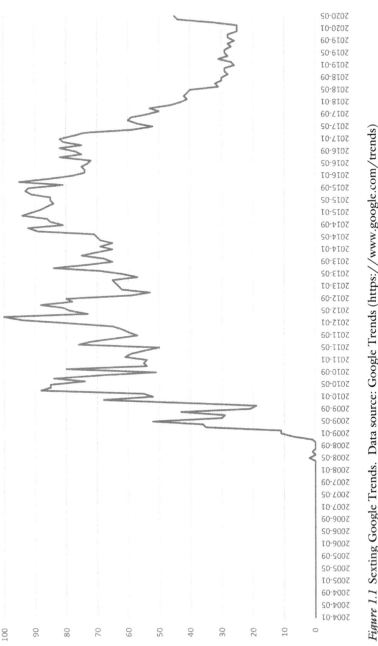

Figure 1.1 Sexting Google Trends. Data source: Google Trends (https://www.google.com/trends)

Figure 1.2 "Revenge pornography" Google Trend. Data source: Google Trends (https://www.google.com/trends)

- S67 2015 Serious Crime Act[14] (extending legislation to include sexual communication with a child)

The use of legislation around teen sexting focuses on the act of manufacturing and distribution of an indecent image of a minor, with little in the legislation to consider the "self-generated" nature of the content.

The foundation of the legislation, the Protection of Children Act 1978, makes it illegal for someone to generate and distribute an indecent image of a child. Clearly, in the event of self-generation and sharing, the victim will also be the perpetrator under this legislation. The legislation was introduced and debated in a time before the day could be envisioned where someone might self-generate an intimate image of themselves from their bedroom and have it passed around may recipients with the touch of a button. However, in the modern digital world, there is a legislation tension between, on the one hand, protecting the victim, and on the other hand, addressing the illegality of the generation and sharing.

For revenge pornography, the major pieces of legislation are newer and on the face of it far more straightforward:

- In England, s33 of the Criminal Justice and Courts Act 2015[15]
- In Scotland, the Abusive Behaviour and Sexual Harm (Scotland) Act 2016[16]

The focus of this legislation is harm to the victim and proof of intent to cause harm, as well as actually sharing the image or video. The Scottish legislation also makes provision for the threat of distribution, a very important addition that will be discussed at far great length throughout the book.

Furthermore, privacy and copyright law have been used to challenge revenge pornography-like behaviours – copyright for a self-generated image will reside with the taker of the image. This has, in the past, been described as "the best weapon against revenge pornography".[17] The US Digital Millennium and Copyright Act has been used frequently for "takedowns" where abusers have posted messages to public platforms such as social media sites.[18] Given many of these platforms reside in the US, this is the most effective and timely way to have images removed before there is a risk of further redistribution. However, this is a "best fit" tool that again fails to acknowledge that many of the images and other

14 UK Government (2015). "Section 67, Serious Crime Act 2015". http://www.legislation.gov.uk/ukpga/2015/9/section/67
15 Ibid.
16 UK Government (2016). "Abusive Behaviour and Sexual Harm (Scotland) Act 2016". http://www.legislation.gov.uk/asp/2016/22/contents/enacted
17 Levenndoski, Amanda (2014). "Our Best Weapon Against Revenge Porn: Copyright Law?". https://www.theatlantic.com/technology/archive/2014/02/our-best-weapon-against-revenge-porn-copyright-law/283564/
18 Levendowski, A. (2013). "Using copyright to combat revenge porn". *NYU journal of Intellectual Property and Entertainment Law*, 3, 422.

media used for abuse may not have been taken by the subject of the image and we will present a number of case studies that show covert image capture and consensual capture by a partner can also result in the sharing of material from which a victim might be subject to abuse. While copyright legislation is a useful tool for the takedown of media, the abuse and harm cannot be addressed.

Through research and policy analysis, this text will show that there is clearly a need for legislation to protect victims. However, it will also explore whether, of itself, legislation is the solution to protecting victims and whether, in some cases, particularly with young people, the legislation is actually resulting in re-victimisation and the potential criminalisation of victims. A perennial example of this ties back into the mantra "don't sext, it's illegal".

While this book looks far more broadly than the prevention of sharing of indecent images by children, these two explorations of the views of adult stakeholders on digital safeguarding and "safety" are useful to place in the context of both the drivers of the legislative process around sexting and revenge pornography and also to reflect upon the language used in this space when forming opinion, policy and media copy. In our work, we see that public discourse is generally beset with the following:

- Gut reactions as fact – statements by senior police and politicians that are little more than opinion but stated as fact
- Authority without evidence – a belief if something is said with enough conviction, the need for evidence is diminished, for example, "technology exists to solve this" when it clearly does not
- Threats of criminalisation – don't do it, it's illegal
- Victim blaming – "if they didn't take the image in the first place, it wouldn't be shared"
- Monitoring and technological solutions – technology is the answer, it caused it; therefore it should prevent it as well

Using media headlines by way of example:

- *Sexting among teens is out of control: "'Sexting pandemic' in Ipswich and Suffolk as paedophiles hide on social media"*[19]
- *All teens are engaged in sexting: "Sext Texts Epidemic: Experts warn sharing explicit photos is corrupting children"*[20]

19 Hirst, A. (2018). "'Sexting pandemic' in Ipswich and Suffolk as paedophiles hide on Social Media". *East Anglian Daily Times.* http://www.eadt.co.uk/news/sexting-pandemic-in-ipswich-and-suffolk-as-paedophiles-hide-on-social-media-1-5229502
20 Martin, D (2012). "Sex Texts Epidemic: Experts Warn Sharing Explicit Photos is Corrupting Children". *The Daily Mail.* http://www.dailymail.co.uk/news/article-2246154/Sex-texts-epidemic-Experts-warn-sharing-explicit-photos-corrupting-children.html

- *Very young children as sexting:* "*Children as young as seven caught sexting at school, study reveals*"[21]
- *Revenge pornography isn't problematic behaviour:* "*Do YOU endorse revenge porn? Shocking study shows that 99% of people support the practice*"[22]
- *Revenge pornography and celebrity:* "*Revenge porn: some of the biggest celebrity victims*"[23]

The discourse can be shown to focus on the technology, the act and the sexual nature of the exchange. Given the public discourse and attitudes of stakeholders in online child safeguarding, perhaps it should not be surprising when young people share these attitudes. What is seen far less in public discourse are things like the youth voice or any empathy related to the victim. In order to understand the broader context of sending self-produced intimate images, perhaps talking to those who carry out such practices might give a better understanding than conjecture and opinion? However, as with most policy direction, which ultimately leads to legislation, those who are actually engaged in the sort of practices in which they wish to mitigate risk are generally those who have the least heard voice in the debate. Policy focuses on trying to ensure young people do not send intimate images of themselves to others, with a resultant policy focus that places pressure on industry to "do more" or produce legislation that will prohibit such practices. If there was a better understanding of motivations for both those who take and initially share images, and those who choose to share those images further, perhaps policy might be better able to develop legislation that will help victims, rather than the current position were many victims are too scared to disclose harm or abuse that arises from the non-consensual sharing of images they have taken. Research conducted by authors with the UK Safer Internet Centre, the Australian eSafety Commissioner's Office and Netsafe New Zealand, discussed in far more detail later in this text,[24] illustrate this clearly via the youth voice, with one 16-year-old female expressing with some upset how the legal message delivered in schools means that if a minor is being abused as a result of sending a nude, they will not ask for help, which will have a negative impact on their mental health and wellbeing.

21 Weale, S. (2016). "Children as young as Seven Caught sexting at school, Study Reveals". *The Guardian.* https://www.theguardian.com/society/2016/mar/25/children-young-se ven-caught-sexting-school-study-reveals
22 Lloyd, P (2017). "Do you endorse revenge porn? Shocking study shows that 99% of people support the practice - and they're probably psychopaths!". *The Daily Mail.* https://ww w.dailymail.co.uk/sciencetech/article-4277710/Most-people-ENDORSE-use-revenge-po rn.html
23 Perry, K (2014). "Revenge porn: some of the biggest celebrity victims". *The Telegraph.* https ://www.telegraph.co.uk/news/celebritynews/11129357/Revenge-porn-some-of-the -biggest-celebrity-victims.html
24 UK Safer Internet Centre (2017). "Young People and Sexting – Attitudes and Behaviours. Research Findings from the United Kingdom, New Zealand and Australia". https://swgfl. org.uk/Uploads/1b/1bb7d65b-b6a7-4c55-81bc-aef5de6bcb59.pdf

This comment is fundamental to the arguments presented throughout this book – it shows how victims are repeatedly failed when attempts to protect them are enmeshed in legislation being used in a manner for which it was never intended, as well as highlighting the broader context of an intimate "selfie" – the victim might have been pressured into sending the image, and once the image has been sent, there might be subsequent forms of abuse. Legislation, and educational messages, are failing to protect victims of abuse because, legislatively speaking, they have done something wrong. By failing to understand the broader context around the generation and sending of images, victims feel even more isolated and scared to ask for help. Even advice for schools fails to address the complexities around the act of generation, distribution and potential redistribution of an image.

The whole phenomenon of non-consensual sharing of intimate images has been beset by failures to explore wider causal factors and impacts upon victims. Even the terms "self-produced", "self-generated" and "youth-produced" sexual imagery are problematic, suggesting that the image was voluntarily produced by the taker with no consideration of coercion, exploitation or pressure. In the recent international work across the UK, Australia and New Zealand,[26] 70% of UK young people said that pressure was a key factor in people sending nudes. These definitions facilitating victimisation and a culture of victim blaming that will be prevalent throughout this text.

It is these issues that form the central theme of this book – the tension between legislation and social behaviour are such that while the intention of the legislation might be to protect victims, it is not sufficient in order to achieve this. Moreover, in some cases, the legislation is being used to punish, rather than help, victims.

However, there is also a broader exploration in this book that marries empirical data with a more philosophical perspective on the role legislation has to play in a society and where, in the case of sexting and revenge pornography, this is the case. While scholars have debated the nuance on the role of law in society for many years, a fundamental agreement exists that law is, in essence, a set of rules on which society agrees (generally democratically) in order to regulate behaviour,[25] such that, through statute, the state protects the rights of its citizens. Therefore, in order to consider the role of legislation around acts such as sexting and revenge pornography, one would expect it to ensure that rights to privacy and reputation are upheld and protection from abuse is ensured. However, throughout this text, questions will be raised whether legislation in this field is fit for this purpose and explore, through empirical evidence, where the law can be found lacking. Furthermore, by the exploration of how, as a result of the limitations of legislation (and, arguably, therefore governments) to protect individuals, policy direction becomes in essence finger-pointing and the passing of expectation and responsibility.

25 Robertson, Geoffrey (2006). "Crimes Against Humanity". Penguin.

Legislative and Social Dimensions of Image-Based Abuse

In exploring these themes, the book is broken into three sections. The first, Chapters 2 and 3, will explore the broader content of teen sexting and revenge pornography as a context in which to place the legislative exploration. Drawing from extensive empirical work conducted by the authors, these chapters will go some way to illustrating the complex social discourse around these two overlapping phenomena.

A number of primary data sources will be used to empirically explore the broad social issues around image-based abuse. From the teen sexting perspective, there is survey data that reached approximately 2000 children and young people. Additionally, there is a wealth of discussion data with young people on attitudes to sexting and addressing their questions on the topic from the many visits to schools to work over ten years. In total, transcripts detailing discussions with over 500 young people aged between 14 and 16 have been used in this analysis. All of these discussions, conducted by one of the authors of this text, were carried out in a classroom environment with parental consent and trusted teaching staff present. While these sessions were approached with some trepidation when first conducted, given the sensitive nature of the topic, what was soon discovered was this was something young people wanted to talk about and to ask questions and get clear and unambiguous answers. What is also very apparent from the discussions, which are drawn upon throughout the text, both attitudes and the questioning nature of young people have not changed during the ten years in which this research has been conducted.

The other major source of primary data is drawn from the Revenge Porn Helpline[26] casebook, which has been accessed over the duration of this project. The Revenge Porn Helpline was launched in February 2015 with the specific mandate of assisting and advising people who have been the victim of revenge pornography. The Helpline is provided by South West Grid for Learning (SWGfL) Trust, a not-for-profit charitable trust with a long history of working with schools in the "online safety" space, providing them with both technological interventions and education and training to help them contribute to safer online worlds for children and young people. One aspect of the trust's work was a Professionals Online Safety Helpline which supported those in the children's workforce with advice around online safety incidents they had encountered. As a result of the knowledge developed by the trust, and their support in the emerging legislation around revenge pornography, the trust received funding from the UK government to provide the new Revenge Porn Helpline. The helpline comprises a small team of professionals who provide telephone and online support for victims of revenge pornography and help them resolve issues arising from the non-consensual sharing of images.

26 https://revengepornhelpline.org.uk/

As well as access to the casebook, comprising over 3000 calls and contacts to the helpline, empirical work involved interviews with staff on the helpline. This provided the means to explore the grassroots nature of image-based abuse among adults to determine things such as:

- Demography and impact on victims
- Location of shared images
- Associated behaviours of offenders alongside the sharing of images
- Attitudes of offenders
- "Types" of revenge pornography
- Response by other agencies (law enforcement, etc.)

The work with the Revenge Porn Helpline is also utilised in later chapters of this book when consideration is made regarding what might be done to develop legislation and how victims can best be supported.

The second section of the book will explore legislation in more detail. While the focus of this legislation is the UK, as this is where the majority of the empirical work has been conducted, parallels will be drawn with other jurisdictions to show the differences and similarities of approaches. There is also an exploration of sentencing to date and existing case law to show both the successes of legislation and the challenges it faces.

The final third of the book will marry up the first two sections by further drawing upon empirical work with a focus on the victim. In addition, it explores stakeholder and rights perspectives in more detail to show the need for engagement beyond legislation and for social policy to be more progressive in its approach. It will explore the role specifically of service providers, given the focus on them as "solution architects" to these issues and how they respond as a result of threats of stronger legislation. It will also return to the themes introduced in this opening chapter – that prohibition is not an answer and technology cannot provide solutions to social problems. The text concludes by calling for a more progressive approach to these issues, for legislation to be effective in supporting the stakeholder community and for this community to be aware of the issues faced by victims of these crimes so they can be supported, rather than judged.

Author Contributions

This text brings together different perspectives and thinking on image-based abuse from the academic and legal world. The majority of the empirical work in this text is drawn from the work of Phippen, with academic support from Brennan. The authors thank Jocelyn Ledward and Jennifer Agate for their input into Chapters 4 and 5. Views expressed within the text, drawn from the empirical work, do not necessarily represent the views of all contributing authors.

2 Sexting in Context

In Chapter 1, it was stated that in order to be able to legislate effectively, one needs to first understand the social context in which the legislation is set. If the policy focus fails to do that, the legislation, and its subsequent interpretation, will struggle to be applied in the manner it has been intended. However, perhaps worse than this is when legislation, developed for one purpose, is used for another. One of the worst examples of this in the post-digital world is teen sexting, a cultural phenomenon that, as discussed in Chapter 1, is very much an act that has emerged through the prevalence of the mobile phone, particularly those with cameras in them.

In this chapter we explore the "grassroots" of teen sexting in more detail, drawing from extensive research in the field, working with young people themselves and also stakeholders in the child safeguarding domain to present a broader view of the phenomenon. This is done prior to the presentation and analysis of the legislation because the flaws in the legislative approach are clearer once the context has been explored. It is too easy to view teen sexting as something where a minor chooses to send an intimate image of themselves to someone else (for the sake of argument, also a minor), without exploring the bigger picture in the exchange. If it is, quite rightly, decided that, as a society, we do not want minors taking intimate images of themselves and sending them to others, but do not wish to explore their motivations (and whether there were any coercive elements in the production of the image), it can simply be stated, "we need to stop young people doing this". Then, existing legislation that might apply can be explored for its efficacy, or new legislation can be created, in order to prevent this – let's stop teens sexting. The focus of policymakers lies in prohibitive actions and while it may be viewed that the role of legislation should be in protecting victims and punishing offenders, the legislative approach (which will be explored in far more detail in Chapter 4) presents a number of challenges when addressing behaviours underpinned by, and arguably normalised and legitimised through, online platforms.

Putting a Stop to Teen Sexting

Even the term is something of a creation at odds with the behaviours young people engage with and observe in their peers. A key fact that comes through very strongly from discussion with young people is that "sexting" is rarely used as a term by young people – they will generally refer to "nudes" and "dick pics". The distinction between the two is clear for young people. For dick pics, it relates to the practice where some boys will "volunteer" a photograph of their genitals as part of a "courtship ritual" – as a way to "ask out" a girl. For nudes, our empirical work over the years has highlighted that it is clear girls are far less likely to volunteer images like this; however, they may send "nudes" as part of a relationship or in response to requests (sometimes repeated and persistent) from a boy. These are certainly not the only two scenarios that will result in the generation of teen sexting images, but they are the two that are well known and result in the "nudes and dick pics" terminology.

As such, it should be stressed that "sexting" is an often used and poorly understood term. It aims to categorise a wide range of behaviours, from the voluntary sharing of an image to one that has been coerced by a peer or extorted from an adult abuser. Yet the focus of policymakers and legislators, as is discussed throughout this book, seems to be the actual act of exchanging an image of itself, rather than understanding the motivations and broader context for doing so.

Equally, terms such as "youth-produced indecent images" imply a voluntary engagement with the production and distribution of the image, and do little to move the policy focus from "victim blaming" (another problematic term) and prohibition towards supporting the rights of the child. When reflecting specifically on the rights of the abused towards the end of this book, this is something which will be explored in more detail. However, for now, it is worthwhile to acknowledge the fact that both legislation and policy language does imply fault on the taker (and usually subject) of the image, with little consideration of the surrounding context within which the image (or video) is taken. In recent international work across the UK, Australia and New Zealand, NOTEREF _Ref511412117 \h * MERGEFORMAT [3] 70% of UK young people said that pressure was a key factor in people sending nudes. These definitions facilitate victimisation and a culture of blame that will be prevalent throughout this book.

Finding a youth voice is essential in this area – there are many adults who believe they know what young people are doing and have the solution to ensuring young people do not engage in these practices. However, they rarely actually listen to what young people have to say. A consistent response over many years of our empirical work when asking young people what are the best things adults can do to help them in the event of harm or abuse arising from the sharing of images is "listening" and "not judging".

To quote the US researcher danah boyd:[1]

teen sexting is a very rational act with very irrational consequences.

---

1 boyd, danah (2011). "Teen Sexting and Its Impact on the Tech Industry". *Read Write Web 2WAY Conference*. New York, NY, 13 June.

It is a very sensible summary of the act and fallout from the act. In an environment where young people believe that attractiveness is a highly desirable quality, that being in a relationship is an important part of knowing you are attractive and with the means to take "selfies" and send them easily, why wouldn't they engage in these practices? Yet the irrationality of the consequences can be significant – rapid and uncontrolled redistribution, posting online, seen by thousands – is something new to this phenomenon. It is this part of the act that differs from generational similarities for the desire to be in a relationship or to be told one is attractive. It is complicated.

Yet this complexity is rarely seen when exploring information provided by stakeholders or media coverage of teen sexting events. Everyone seems to have an opinion on why people choose to disclose intimate images and the motivations for the non-consensual sharing of intimate images among minors and adults. A perennial example of this ties back into the mantra "don't sext, it's illegal".

The legislation is clear – anyone taking an indecent image of a child (defined in law to be anyone under the age of 18) is breaking the law, regardless of whether they have that image in their possession or they distribute it further. Therefore, anyone "self-generating" an intimate image is breaking this law, regardless of whether they forward the image to others. Anyone receiving the image will be breaking the law, regardless of whether they forward the image to others.

Having spoken to many young people in the course of the empirical work explored in this book, many have said that they have been told that taking and sending an explicit self-generated image is illegal. While the nuance of this legality is explored in far more detail later in this book, and according to the above legislation, the messages are correct, they are also inaccurate, incomplete and unhelpful. While the empirical work explored in this book goes back over ten years (engaging in initial work, discussed below, in 2008), it would seem that these messages persist. By way of an example, a social media post in March 2018 by a UK regional police force[2] made a point of reiterating the message of illegality.

Advice by the UK's National Society for the Prevention of Cruelty to Children (NSPCC) on sexting carries a similar warning:[3]

> Sexting can be seen as harmless, but creating or sharing explicit images of a child is illegal, even if the person doing it is a child. A young person is breaking the law if they:
>
> take an explicit photo or video of themselves or a friend
> share an explicit image or video of a child, even if it's shared between children of the same age

2 https://www.facebook.com/DevonAndCornwallPolice/photos/a.10150903636467988.
432838.151265442987/10156081376332988/
3 NSPCC (n.d.). "Sexting". https://www.nspcc.org.uk/preventing-abuse/keeping-children-s
afe/sexting/

possess, download or store an explicit image or video of a child, even if the child gave their permission for it to be created.

While the advice on the NSPCC website continues to say:

> However, as of January 2016 in England and Wales, if a young person is found creating or sharing images, the police can choose to record that a crime has been committed but that taking formal action isn't in the public interest.

This point, which relates to outcome 21 recording of crimes associated with section 1 of the Protection of Children Act 1978, is explored in greater detail later in this text, as while it was viewed as a positive step forwards, there are still implications for young people in the use of this approach.

Again, this information is still incomplete and ambiguous in its language and provides little reassurance to a minor who has, for example, been coerced into producing an intimate image of themselves and sent it to their abuser and is subsequently scared to tell anyone because they have been told that what they have done is illegal. This is not a pragmatic application of legislation for ensuring that victims are protected and abusers are punished. This is people within the safeguarding stakeholder group not wishing to tackle the complexities of the issue and hiding behind (inadequate and out of date) legislation.

Coupled with a failure to address social concerns while hiding behind legislation, deflection around issues of online harm which places an expectation that because technology has facilitated a social problem, technology should be able to mitigate against it, is prevalent. In addressing this popular policy approach, a statement made by a senior UK politician will be explored later in this text as a demonstration once more of the application of the "do more" policy approach used by many politicians trying to deflect from their own responsibilities.

Doing more for teen sexting

Legislation, and educational messages, are failing to protect victims of abuse because, legislatively speaking, they have done something wrong. By failing to understand the broader context around the generation and sending of images, victims feel even more isolated and scared to ask for help. Even advice for schools fails to address the complexities around the act of generation, distribution and potential redistribution of an image. In the UK Council for Child Internet Safety advice to schools on sexting,[4] which purports to provide guidance for school

---

4 UKCCIS (2016). "Sexting in schools and colleges: Responding to incidents and safeguarding young people". https://assets.publishing.service.gov.uk/government/uploads/system/upl oads/attachment_data/file/609874/6_2939_SP_NCA_Sexting_In_Schools_FINAL_Upd ate_Jan17.pdf

leaders and safeguarding professions on safeguarding young people in the event of sexting incidents, the opening statement around the law states:

> Much of the complexity in responding to youth produced sexual imagery is due to its legal status. Making, possessing and distributing any imagery of someone under 18 which is "indecent" is illegal. This includes imagery of yourself if you are under 18.
>
> The relevant legislation is contained in the Protection of Children Act 1978 (England and Wales) as amended in the Sexual Offences Act 2003 (England and Wales).
>
> Specifically:
>
> • It is an offence to possess, distribute, show and make indecent images of children.
> • The Sexual Offences Act 2003 (England and Wales) defines a child, for the purposes of indecent images, as anyone under the age of 18.

However, another paragraph stands out:

> If a young person has shared imagery consensually, such as when in a romantic relationship, or as a joke, and there is no intended malice, it is usually appropriate for the school to manage the incident directly. In contrast, any incidents with aggravating factors, for example, a young person sharing someone else's imagery without consent and with malicious intent, should generally be referred to police and/or children's social care. If you have any doubts about whether to involve other agencies, you should make a referral to the police.

This document is used by the UK Department for Education as official guidance on how schools should deal with sexting and used extensively by schools as their "go to" document when dealing with sexting incidents. The paragraph seems like a let-off for someone who might argue that while they did share an image, they did not do it to cause offence, something that will be returned to in our exploration of legislation and policy around the concept of "distress". What happens, in this context, when the victim is upset as a result of the shared image, but the sharer of the image says they did it as a joke? Even in a case where there was no malicious intent on the part of the sharer (although one might doubt the motivations to share an intimate image of a peer if they claimed it wasn't to cause harm or distress), surely the focus of harm should be on the victim, not the sharer? Again, by failing to understand the broader context in the production and sharing of an indecent image, the policy direction fails the victim. And, again, the premise of intent to cause harm or upset will be returned to at many times in this text.

An empirical history of teen sexting

The following details a journey in understanding the sexting phenomenon through research in the exchange of indecent images among minors, and surrounding behaviours since 2008. During that time, we have undertaken surveys with around 2000 young people in two major projects (2009 and 2017) and some of the statistics from those will be drawn out below. In addition, and, in our opinion more importantly, since that time we have spoken with thousands of children. These discussions may take place in assemblies, classrooms, workshops and focus groups, and can explore issues around attitudes towards youth involved imagery, its prevalence, the impact of legislation, educational approach and the role of stakeholders in keeping young people safe.

The start of this journey was 2008 when a programme of work with an NGO called the South West Grid for Learning[5] was commenced. The aim of this work was to determine the prevalence of "sexting" among Key Stage 4 (14–16) young people. The motivation for this research was frequent visits to schools where senior leaders expressed concern at having to deal with a "sexting" incident and not knowing what to do about it. Given another part of this research was, and still is, advocacy with policymakers to raise awareness of online issues faced by children and young people, these observations were communicated to the policy world. However, the general response was one of disbelief that this was such a prevalent issue. Therefore, it was decided to engage in research to try to measure the problem.

It is worthwhile reflecting upon the direction of survey work in this area – there is a policy obsession with "how many young people do this" which is counterproductive and very difficult to measure. Given the focus of most education in this area is to remind young people that engaging in such practice is illegal, it is very unlikely there will be an honest response from young people when asked, "do you send nudes?" There is also an ethical issue arising from asking children to disclose if they have "self-generated" an image, given that, by the letter of the law, this is illegal.

Therefore, the focus of the research has always been around the culture of youth involved imagery – it explores how young people are exposed to this material, whether they are affected by it and what their thoughts are about both those who generate material and those who share/spread it.

The early survey work in 2009,[6] which ultimately resulted in data collected from just over 1000 14–16-year-olds, asked about awareness of images and attitudes around these images, as a means to measure how many young people are affected by "sexting".

As an immediate observation on prevalence, a discussion group with the "senior" (i.e. Key Stage 4, aged 14–16) pupils from the school council at a secondary setting in the south-west of the UK was arranged. This group was used to pilot survey questions and see whether they felt they were appropriate to ask young people of their age. They were told that the aim of the research was to explore teen attitudes and experiences of "sexting". None of the young people spoken to were aware of the term (already highlighting the difference in discourse between young people and adult stakeholders). However, when it was explained what was meant by this, one of the members of the group said:

Oh yeah, that happens all the time here.

From this one comment, it was apparent the survey was timely and the aim to conduct the research was justified. Survey respondents were asked whether they knew people who self-generated and shared indecent images, and around 40% of our respondents said they did. When asked about prevalence, 7% said incidents happened "regularly" and 13% said, "it happens all of the time". The most popular response for this was they were aware of "one or two" incidents of sexting in the last year (almost 40%).

One other important early detail to consider was determining how often images were shared beyond the intended recipient. This measure was influenced by a conversation with the small group of year-10 (aged 14–15) boys, where one observed that most sharing of intimate images was never disclosed; however, it was when the image was spread beyond the intended recipient, often by the intended recipient, that problems arose.

In this early survey, 56% of respondents said they were aware of instances where images were shared further than the intended recipient. However, interestingly, when asked whether they thought that the aim of further spreading was to cause upset, only 22% said they felt this was the case. Which does raise the question of what do they think the intentions of someone to non-consensually share an indecent image of a peer would be? So, even ten years ago, the research showed a population of teenagers who were exposed to the "risks" around sexting – for a minority, it was something they were exposed to "all of the time", much of it went on without any visibility beyond those exchanging the images, and for those who were exposed to images, sometimes it was because someone had shared it, rather than because they had requested it. All of these respondents, through their disclosure, are confessing to engaging with the taking and distribution of indecent images of minors, so criminal in the eyes of the law.

The early survey work was in some way only scratching the surface of understanding behaviours around teen sexting, but it did demonstrate for a lot of young people, this was something they routinely face as part of their world – while perhaps not being directly engaged with self-generation, they would be exposed to images and behaviours that would relate to images of peers. One other point to note is even at this early stage of research, young people were already expressing concerns around the tension between protection and legislation when asked what more could be done by other stakeholders to help, as well as recognising the difference between a consensual and non-consensual exchange.

Following on from the 2009 survey work and its subsequent discussion in schools, such as assemblies and workshops in classes, a lot of young people did not believe the figure of 40% being aware of "self-generation incidents". The vast majority of young people spoken to said that figure would be much higher

– awareness was prevalent, even if those who carried out such acts was smaller. A recurrent theme in the discussion was the difference between being aware of an image (e.g. being sent it by a third party, hearing people talk about it, seeing it on social media) and producing and sending an image themselves. This also harks back to an interesting tension between law and awareness – a recipient may be in possession of an image because it had been forwarded to them (e.g. in a group chat), then retained on the device even though the message was removed. This would still be possession in the eyes of the law.

As a result of "sexting" being a recurring discussion topic with both young people and staff at schools we visited, it was decided that further research was needed in order to spend a focused amount of time talking about these issues. Therefore, in 2012, a further piece of research was embarked upon with the NSPCC[7] that centred around focus groups with young people specifically exploring their attitudes towards these issues and how it impacted their lives. Around 100 young people were spoken to specifically as a result of this piece of research and allowed a detailed exploration of what was emerging from the many assemblies, classes and workshops that were carried out over this period of time. There were a number of key findings that were drawn from this work that again highlighted how the culture of self-generation was impacting upon this generation.

First, and perhaps most importantly given the tension between legislators, safeguarding stakeholders and young people themselves (respectively – "it's illegal, they shouldn't do it", "they are doing it, how can we stop them doing it", "it's going on, can you help those who end up harmed as a result"), there was the mundanity of these practices as perceived by young people spoken to. This is something that happens, people get exposed to the images, whether they want to or not, and those in the images will be subject to either abuse or passivity as a result of a number of factors such as gender, popularity and resilience. A young person who is already vulnerable, perhaps unpopular and already being bullied in some way, would be far more likely to receive abuse as a result of producing and sending an image, whereas someone popular and resilient would frequently laugh it off. Again, this shows that this is something that needs to be dealt with on a case-by-case basis, with the appropriate policy in place, rather than blanket bans and threats of prosecution. There was general agreement that a boy was far more likely to "volunteer" an image to a girl (in general, heterosexual relationships were the focus of discussion) and girls would self-generate as a result of a request or pressure. There was also general agreement that harm and abuse will generally arise as a result of the non-consensual sharing to third parties, rather than the initial production and sharing of the image.

7 Phippen, A. (2012). "Sexting: An exploration of practices, attitudes and influences". https:// library.nspcc.org.uk/HeritageScripts/Hapi.dll/filetransfer/2012SextingExplorationPracti cesAttitudesInfluencesReport.pdf

When considering gender differences with this group, the concept of the voluntary "dick pic" is an interesting one to reflect upon – while one might easily dismiss this as boys behaving in an irresponsible manner, again, this is generally due to prejudice on the part of adult stakeholders who are not willing to explore the underlying causes in more depth. If one unpicks why a boy might volunteer a "dick pic", the motivations are generally less about causing offence or to harass the recipient, but because the boy wished to engage in a relationship with the girl and they believed this was the way to start. One thing that came from a number of the discussions was that, for some boys, there was a belief that this was the way to "ask someone out".

There is a view that might be expressed that they should know better than this and isn't it ridiculous that they think this, but, given the dearth of effective sex and relationships in schools, this knowledge vacuum is filled with peer discussion and "hand me down" information from older friends and siblings. If they know someone older who is seen as successful in forming relationships who has engaged in the sending of "dick pics", or they have seen celebrities engaged in such behaviour, why wouldn't they think this is acceptable behaviour?

To further develop the exploration of education delivered and the discussions with young people around this, what was clear was that none of them had received any meaningful education around self-generation or how they might deal with the fallout from this. Sex education generally centred around biological reproduction and the spreading of STIs. Any coverage of "sexting" was generally delivered in assemblies and would be prohibitive, rather than educative. The closest any young person came to discussing self-generation practices was being told that it was illegal and you shouldn't do it – an often delivered mantra was "once it's online, there's nothing you can do about it" which, when reflected upon, can be an extremely distressing message to deliver to, for example, a 13-year-old child who has just learned that everyone in their year group has seen an image of them naked. There was no acknowledgement from any education received that something can be done in the event of an image being shared, or that this is something that, sadly, is tackled by schools on a daily basis across the country. Prohibition, it seemed, was the driving force behind what meagre "education" the young people did receive around sexting.

Perhaps as a result of this lack of empathy and knowledge by adult stakeholders in these young people's safeguarding, it seemed unsurprising that most believed that these issues should be dealt with at a peer level, preferably not involving adults. In fact, it was viewed that adults should only be included in any approach to resolution. For most young people, the advice they would give peers is to work through the upset because shame is transient. In a few weeks, someone else would be the focus of ridicule and abuse. Furthermore, from most of these discussions, the locus of blame resided with the person who had taken the image. There was little sympathy for those who had their images shared wider – "if they hadn't taken the image, it couldn't be shared". Any challenge to this, such as suggesting that perhaps the main fault lay with the person who had chosen to share the image non-consensually, generally the responses was still "yes, but if they hadn't made the image in the first place...".

Updating Youth Views of Sexting

Over the subsequent four years, while no specific empirical research was embarked upon to look at sexting per se, work in schools highlighted that self-generation was not going away and it was also perhaps trickling down in term of the age of those engaging with the practices. It was also apparent that attitudes towards victims of abuse and where blame lay had changed very little. Therefore, it was decided that a further round of detailed research should be commenced with both a quantitative and qualitative element to determine what had changed and whether quantifiable measures were similar. This work was conducted with the UK Safer Internet Centre alongside the Office of the eSafety Commissioner in Australia and Netsafe in New Zealand. This transnational project was conducted to compare behaviours in three westernised cultures.[8]

Unsurprisingly, there was little change in statistics between the 2009 and 2017 surveys (even though respondents from the 2017 survey were, on average, two years younger than in 2009), with 49% of a respondent population of 750 young people reporting knowledge of self-generated images; 19% said that they were aware of "a few" incidents in the past year, and 12% said it "happens all the time". Knowledge of further spreading was admitted by 44% of the population, with 68% of respondents saying they didn't think this was done to cause upset. In contrast to the 2009 survey, questions were added around motivations. Previous research had highlighted that the practice was common. However, there was far less understanding of motivations and root causes from producing an intimate image of oneself. When asked about motivation, 67% thought people sent nudes because they wanted a relationship, 68% to be told they were attractive and 66% because they were pressured into doing it. Pressure is a significant issue that occurs when talking to victims of both minor and adult victims of non-consensual sharing of intimate images and one we will return to at length.

There were many other parallels with the 2009 data set, particularly related to victim blaming. Almost 70% of respondents said that did not believe that images shared non-consensually by a third party would be done so to cause upset and over 70% said the responsibility for the image lay with the person who took it. Less than 10% saw any responsibility for the recipient of the image.

The influence of the prohibitive approach to education was also very clear; 64% of respondents agreed to some level with the statement "Sending nudes is illegal and people shouldn't do it". Interestingly, more felt those who spread images further are subject to illegality, with 83% agreeing with the statement "Spreading a nude is to other people is illegal and people shouldn't do it". This contrasts sharply with the attitude that most do not spread nudes to cause upset. Perhaps most significantly for discussions later in this book, almost as many also

---

8 UK Safer Internet Centre (2017). "Young People and Sexting – Attitudes and Behaviours. Research Findings from the United Kingdom, New Zealand and Australia". https://swgfl.org.uk/Uploads/1b/1bb7d65b-b6a7-4c55-81bc-aef5de6bcb59.pdf

agreed with the statement "People should be punished for threatening to share images", with 76% agreeing with this. Yet the law that is applied to "child protection" in teen sexting has no provision for such eventualities.

Crucially, in terms of the role adults with a responsibility for child welfare have in these scenarios, when asked what they can do most to help, 72% of young people said they wanted "safe spaces" to be able to get advice without the threat of punishment (harking back to a comment made by a respondent in 2009); 74% said "don't judge", 76% said "listen" and 70% said "have open and honest conversations". There were comments from young people that acknowledged the disproportionate nature of the legal response to the behaviour, and also the need for adults with a responsibility for safeguarding to understand the upset the young person is experiencing, rather than coming out with the mantra:

You shouldn't have done that, it's illegal.

As ever, the qualitative element provided far more detail to the discussion. Carried out with 100 year-10 young people from seven different schools, what was clear was there was a belief that these behaviours are getting younger. A lot of respondents (all aged between 14 and 15) stated that self-generation was something that had "died down" in their year; however, it had taken place when they were younger. Interestingly, they were also concerned that, for example, a year-8 child might self-generate, even though when they were that age it went on! Which does highlight how quickly a judgemental viewpoint develops among people who have previously been exposed to these behaviours.

Perhaps one of the clearest things to emerge from the discussions was how little attitudes have changed over the past five years. Attitudes were still mundane, education was still sparse and tended to be in an "output only" form (see below), and knowledge was still developed by peers. It seemed that regardless of the activity of the online safety community and numerous resources being developed to help schools "teach" issues around self-generation, the reality was this was having zero impact on children. While Chapter 7 explores rights in far greater detail, it is worth reflecting upon the UN Convention on the Rights of the Child[9] Article 29 – the Goals of Education at this stage. Is education being provided that will allow young people to develop "personality, talents and abilities to the fullest"? By failing to provide them with relevant, up to date and pragmatic education around issues such as self-generation, young people are left to their own devices. Therefore, is it any wonder they engage in risky behaviours and think the way to engage in a relationship is to share images of their genitals or ask for intimate images of their peers?

---

9 The United Nations (1989). "The United Nations Convention on the Rights of the Child". https://downloads.unicef.org.uk/wp-content/uploads/2016/08/unicef-convention-rig hts-child-uncrc.pdf?_ga=2.250979654.1906569044.1589201424-1114156713.158920 1424

However, there were a number of new, emerging, issues coming from the 2017–2019 discussions that were not explored in detail in the previous research. The first, as mentioned above, is the decreasing age of those engaging in self-generation. In one case, a primary school disclosed that they had to deal with an incident where an 11-year-old boy had sent his "girlfriend" an indecent image. While this is an alarming thing to hear in the first instance, with reflection, is it surprising that younger children are seeing this as part of a relationship? The dearth of education around relationships, particularly in the primary setting, has already been mentioned. In discussions with primary school teachers in staff training sessions and conferences, this is not an isolated incident. While it would not be right to say the sexting incidents in primary schools are now common, it is something many have had to face on occasion, and therefore, should be mindful that policy and training is in place, as well as education in the classroom, to address this.

One thing that was explored in far more detail with these discussions was the role pressure plays in self-generation. The survey work showed that a lot of young people believed pressure was one of the main reasons people took and shared nudes. This was certainly confirmed in our discussion groups, with many young people talking about persistent demands for images or feeling peer pressure to engage in these practices. What was also apparent was that many young people could not see anything wrong with being subjected to this sort of pressure which, if interpreted as some described in groups, might be viewed more seriously as coercion or harassment. Where an individual is sending many messages per day asking for a nude image or, in worse cases, using previously obtained images to demand more, often increasingly explicit, pictures or videos, clearly this is behaviour that requires the intervention of law enforcement in order to protect victims. However, when both coercer and victim do not see anything wrong with what is happening (because they've never received any effective relationships education on such things) it becomes very difficult for young people to check their behaviours or ask for intervention. If, as has been seen from many years of research, the sender of the image believes that anything that happens subsequently is their fault because they should not have sent the image in the first place, they are unlikely to make a complaint if they are being coerced, even if they recognise the coercion taking place.

However, the role of peer pressure, in general, should also not be underestimated – this is, for many, part of forming relationships. They have seen other peers engage in these practices and are now in relationships. Therefore, in their interpretation, this is a successful technique to achieve a relationship, and this is something that is of paramount importance for a lot of young people. Being in a relationship means one is popular and attractive, two things that carry great currency in their lives. A particular comment from one discussion illustrates the illogical approach some young people have to the formation of relationships and the use of self-generation therein. When asked why boys chose to voluntarily send dick pics, one young man (aged 14) said he thought it was because they would get a nude back. When asked whether that ever worked, he was clear that it did not. When pressed on the matter, he reflected that perhaps one day it might be the case, not whether it's a reasonable thing to do.

The young man went on to explain that the exchange of nudes is what happens at the start of a relationship, in his view, the first step. While this might seem a very strange process for adults, why would he not think this if he only has his peers to learn from and some of those have relationships as a result of this approach?

Don't Send Nudes – It's Illegal

Awareness of legislation was also discussed in more detail with these groups and most young people talked about how "sending a nude is illegal". This seems counterintuitive to the fact that every young person spoken to had been exposed to the fallout from nudes being spread around their schools – surely if they are all aware of the legislation, they would not do it and they would report others that did? Although that logic would only follow If the threat of prosecution was an effective prohibition to such practices.

However, what was clearly apparent was that, as with the majority of "online safety" education that adopts a prohibitive approach, young people are happy to repeat verbatim the messages they have been told – in the same way, we know cyberbullying is a big problem in schools, even discussions with primary aged children will result in them telling you cyberbullying is bad and people should not do it. With "output only" educational approaches – generally being shown videos in assemblies or having a teacher deliver some resources in the classroom – the messages are delivered and can be repeated, but the belief in the message is less clear. Lots of young people say, "don't cyberbully". However, when asked to explain cyberbullying, they struggle. The knowledge is shallow and fragile, unexpectedly, and they are merely repeating what they have been told.

Further discussion around legislation in the focus groups highlighted this further – they have been told self-generation among minors is illegal; however, they are not sure why, what laws the legality relates to or the broader legal context around it. They had many questions around the legislation, which is even difficult for someone like me, who has worked in the field for a long time, to explain in a black and white manner, so one must have every sympathy with a teacher trying to explain this. To explain the illegality arising from a 1978 law, updated in 2003, written in a time where self-generation was never envisaged, and then cross-referenced with CPS advice that says most prosecution of minors would fail the public interest test, is not something easily articulated to young people (this is discussed in far more detail in Chapters 3 and 4). This picture is not generally painted fully for them – they are told, either by teachers or external speakers, that it is illegal and if they do it, they "could be in a lot of trouble". And there the message ends. One young woman said that she had experienced an assembly a couple of years earlier when a member of the police came in and, in her words, "scared us to death" about the trouble they could get in if they took nudes, saying that the message being delivered by a member of law enforcement made it even more frightening.

Another group disclosed that a police visitor at the school had told them not to send nudes because it was illegal and a sexual crime, and it would not be removed from a criminal record at the age of majority.

Young people receive no education about protection from harm if an image was spread, the focus was very much on the originator of the image and their potential criminalisation. Returning to the "scary" talk, when asked whether this talk worked, the girl said it didn't because she was aware of peers who did share nudes. When following up on this statement asking why she felt, if they were all scared, that would be the case? The girl simply reflected that one tends not to think about legality when sending a nude.

However, what they had all decided, as a result of the talk, was that there was no way they would ever tell an adult if a friend was experiencing abuse, coercion or exploitation as a result of sharing a nude. The view was that the first response would be a telling off and threat of bringing in the police, some were aware of victims of the spreading of nudes being told off when they had gone for help. So, it is little wonder that young people suffer in silence when dealing with, sometimes, some highly problematic and harmful fall out as a result of sending a nude. When asked what advice they might give to a friend who was being abused as a result of sending a nude, one girl said that the best advice she could give was to suggest the abuse would die down after a while and to hope someone else attracted attention for doing something similar after a few days.

One of the most concerning areas of "sexting" observed from working with young people is that problem of "victim blaming" – someone sends an image, the recipient shares that image, the victim then receives abuse from the wider community because they are a "slut" or a "slag" for sending the image to this one trusted individual. There is little focus on challenging the behaviour of the individual who spread the image further, just the person who took the image. As already mentioned, almost 75% of respondents said the person responsible for the image is the person who took it, even though in many instances that image might have been generated through peer pressure, harassment or coercion.

An interesting case (interesting because in this case the sharers of the images were blamed and prosecuted, not the original taker) that illustrated this is a 2015[10] prosecution of two teenage boys for the possession and indecent images of a minor (although reported as "revenge pornography"). One of the boys was in a relationship with a girl of a similar age and during that time she had sent him as many as 170 images. When their relationship ended, she asked for the images to be destroyed. However, it came to light that the boy (14 at the time) had sent two images to his friend (then 15) in exchange for £10. When the girl was made aware of this, she alerted the police and the boys were arrested. They were both

---

10 Evans, M. (2015). "Boy Becomes Youngest in Britain to be convicted of 'revenge porn' aged 14". *The Telegraph.* https://www.telegraph.co.uk/news/uknews/crime/11383910/Boy-b ecomes-youngest-in-Britain-to-be-convicted-of-revenge-porn-aged-14.html

found guilty and sentenced to 12-month referral orders and were made to pay costs. It is an interesting case because of the blame lying at the feet of the sharer and recipient, rather than the victim. Yet social media commentary at the time still suggested a focus on her. For example, a comment from a poster on social media in response to a local newspaper reporting the story suggested that the victim was at fault for sending the images in the first place and that she had ruined the abuser's lives by doing so.

This victim blaming has been reflected in many workshops and presentations where this case has been discussed. From the outset, it is often difficult to get young people of a similar age to recognise anything that the offenders have done wrong, even when exploring the financial gain from the sale of indecent images of a minor. Generally, both boys and girls in discussion groups will say that fault should lie with the maker of the images. While girls will, in general, be more likely to try at least briefly to see the victim's perspective, they will usually come back to decide "she shouldn't have taken them in the first place". Boys are less likely to even pay lip service to the suffering of the victim, they will draw liability to her very quickly.

Which, one would surmise, is no surprise if the message given is "don't send nudes, it's illegal", without exploring the more complex issues around pressure and coercion. If young people aren't even aware of consent or coercion as concepts, how are they going to understand that consent is contextual? One does not consent to the blanket sharing of an image just because they have shared it with one individual.

Perhaps the most alarming response to this is the shock that someone might be prosecuted for such a crime. The general view is that sharing of images is so frequent (albeit generally without financial benefit) that it is not something that should result in prosecution.

One area that did differ with the 2017–2019 workshops was more discussion around the use of pseudo-sexual imagery of young people – someone would take an image of a peer from a social media platform (for example, Snapchat, Instagram) and superimpose that image onto pornographic material, which is then shared among peers. While this practice was discussed at length in some sessions, this was not viewed in any way as problematic, just "something that happens". In one case, a girl said someone in her tutor group had done this with an image of her and shared it with her and others in the class. The girl and some of her friends thought this was unacceptable and she spoke to her tutor, who said, stifling a laugh, to go and see the assistant head about it. The assistant head acknowledged that it was an unpleasant thing for the boy to have done; however, there was little that they could do now the image had been circulated, he's just be told not to do it again. At no point was there any consideration of the severity of the behaviour or involvement of other stakeholders within a child protection scenario (either parents or law enforcement). Again, with the focus of messaging on "don't take or send nudes", this school was failing to acknowledge that the law is there to protect victims, rather than scare those who might end up as such in the future.

Extensive discussions with young people highlight that legislative "threats" further exacerbate the victim-blaming focus. If the message given to young people is no more complex than "if you do this, you're breaking the law", the victim is already concerned to disclose. Some young people argue, and this is something some of those tasked with responsibilities for their safeguarding might reflect upon, is that legislation is an easy excuse to not engage with the complex reality of teen sexting – why young people do it, the fallout when something goes wrong and the lack of training among adult stakeholders on these issues. It is easier to say "don't do it, it's illegal", rather than "I can understand that you thought by doing this you would enter into a relationship with this individual, and he has broken down trust and failed to gain your consent in sharing further". Referring back to the UKCCIS guidance discussed earlier in this chapter, it is almost like we are giving schools excuses to not face up to the complexities of this task. We are all hoping someone else will deal with it.

Even with the advent of revenge pornography legislation (discussed in the next three chapters), which clearly states that the non-consensual sharing of an image is illegal, therefore offering protection to the victim, safeguarding is not communicated effectively to young people. If a victim, who is suffering abuse, harassment, bullying or exploitation as a result of self-generating an image believes they are suffering harm because it is their "fault" for sending the image in the first place, we are failing to protect children from the potential serious harm that arises from these behaviours. There is clearly a failure to distinguish between a young person engaged in something considered illegal with something that places them at risk. To analogise with two minors engaging in consensual sexual activity, it would be extremely unlikely if a pregnancy had arisen as a result, those with safeguarding responsibility's first response was to tell them they had broken the law and could be subject to prosecution. However, given the online nature of the exchange of nudes, potentially something they would not have experienced while growing up themselves, the view seems more extreme and punitive.

One thing expressed a great deal from a lot of safeguarding professionals (teachers, advisors, police) is that sexting among teens is now "normal" – it is something "they are all doing" and one should therefore not worry about it. Again, this seems like a dereliction of duties. While one might argue a tension between safeguarding and freedom of expression for young people, there is still a need for appropriate protection for those who are victims of crime as a result of these acts. Clearly, there should be no relaxing of legal protections around this phenomenon, however, the law should be aware of the context of the social discourse it aims to tackle, not be used to punish victims, and it should be there to prosecute those who abuse, coerce and exploit as a result of these acts.

The discussions above have highlighted the failure of young people to recognise coercion and exploitation within these scenarios and, instead, a focus on blaming the victim. Drawing from another piece of research,[11] this can be clearly illustrated. In a round of focus groups with this piece of work, coercion was

---

11 Kennedy, C., and Phippen, A. (2017). "Oh you're all children, children do silly things. You'll be fine. Get over it!". *Entertainment Law Review, 2017* 28(6), 191–197.

often discussed, but not recognised, with young men observing that they might demand an image prior to considering entering into a relationship with a peer, or if they did have an image, it might be used to control the taker. One young man even referred to it as "like a blackmail thing", without acknowledging the severity of what they were saying.

One might observe that, in a rush to ensure young people don't "send nudes", the broader and, arguably, more concerning behaviours such as coercion, exploitation and retention of images are not covered at all. Whichever term the adult population chooses to use, exposure to teen sexting is something that happens to many young people, certainly within every secondary school visited as part of this empirical work (many safeguarding leads would disclose that they will deal with at least one or two per week) and an increasing number of primary schools. Given that these behaviours are now well established among young people, legislative approaches that adopt a prohibitive approach have failed in their attempts to curb young people self-generating. Moreover, there has been virtually no change in attitudes over ten years regarding these practices – a focus on victim blaming and an acceptance that if you've sent someone an image, anything that happens subsequently is deserved. Children are being failed in their right to education around these behaviours, and the legislative threat is failing to curtail such acts. It merely criminalises children for doing something the legislation was never written to address. Legislation and safeguarding stakeholders are failing to support victims and deal proportionately with abusers.

In Chapter 3, the complementary, but different, social phenomenon of "revenge pornography" is explored. While there are clear differences (such as a focus on adult victims and legislation implemented specifically to support victims of this abuse), there are many parallels to be drawn, such as focusing on the act of self-generation and sharing rather than exploring the broader motivational factors, as well as the focus on victim blaming.

3 Revenge Pornography in Context

In further developing the context for the exploration of legislation in this space, focusing on its impact, its efficacy and its failing, this chapter differentiates and explores the modern "revenge pornography" phenomenon. As discussed in Chapter 1, this is a more emergent social phenomenon that "teen sexting" and prior to exploring legislation, and the value of legislation in this context, it is worth exploring the similarities and differences, and therefore, the contrasting legislative challenges.

The majority of this chapter will draw from work with the UK's Revenge Porn Helpline,[1] exploring their cases and the impacts of "revenge pornography" on their clients. However, the first part of the chapter more generally explores revenge pornography, particularly the policy discussion that led to the inclusion of legislation in the Criminal Justice and Courts Act 2015 to address the problem, and a more general exploration of the breadth of issues and impacts upon the victim, drawing upon both the limited literature around revenge pornography and primary data with the victims and those who work with the victims.

However, to begin with, there is a need for a clear differentiation between "sexting" and "revenge pornography".

While the difference is not explicit in legislation, for the purposes of this text, the difference lies with the age of the victim. While it would be possible to prosecute someone who either made or distributed indecent images[2] of someone under the age of 18 and they could be prosecuted under "revenge pornography" legislation, it is far more likely that child protection law would take precedence (even though this law is fairly old when used to combat the distribution of images involving minors). As discussed in Chapter 2, it is also possible that the victim of distribution (i.e. the subject of the image) would be prosecuted under child protection legislation, because the law is very clear on the manufacture of indecent images of a minor.

---

1 https://revengepornhelpline.org.uk
2 While the sharing of media might include still images, videos or other media, for the sake of brevity in discussion, we will refer to this broad range as "images".

If the victim is an adult (i.e. aged 18 or above), the legislation focuses very much upon harm to them and their protection. The policy development around the legislation, and its wording in statute, is victim focused and there is no suggestion that, as a result of the legislation, the victim could be prosecuted.

As an aside, it is acknowledged there is activity that might emerge from a revenge pornography incident that might lead to the prosecution of the victim, for example, if the acts recorded could be considered to fall into gross obscenity or extreme pornography. Equally, the tensions in legislation between the age of consent in the UK (16 years old) and the age of majority (18 years old) means that a consenting couple could become criminally liable for prosecution under child protection legislation if they were to record consensual acts. Or, to express it in another way, two 17-year-olds engaged in a consensual sexual act would not be subject to prosecution. However, if they were to photograph or record the said act, they would be liable under the Protection of Children Act 1978. It is little wonder that many teenagers find these inconsistencies confusing, and it could be argued that this reflects legislation that has evolved with little consideration of these matters, perhaps such is the rush sometimes to move to introduce new regulation onto the statute books. As an aside, and not something that will be pursued in later discussions, the role of the "Digital Age of Majority" that has arisen from Article 8 of the General Data Protection Regulation[3] should also be acknowledged. This regulation defines the age by which a minor can consent to the processing of their digital data without parental approval. While the GDPR defines this as 16, member states were able to define a lower age in their own implementation, which the UK did in section 9 of the Data Protection Act 2018.[4] The UK has chosen 13 as the digital age of consent, which is in line with data processing regulations in the US (the Children's Online Privacy Protection Act 1998[5] and used by most social media companies). Therefore, there are three different ages of consent related to digital behaviours – 13, 16 and 18. It is little wonder young people find this confusing.

Nevertheless, the distinction for this text lies in the age of the victim – below the age of majority, it should be referred to as teen sexting, above the age of majority, this becomes revenge pornography. Indeed, the term,"revenge pornography", when applied to the behaviour and victimisation of minors is problematic in itself. There has been much discussion in the last few years over the use of

3 The European Union (2016). "The General Data Protection Regulation 2016". https://eur-lex.europa.eu/legal-content/EN/TXT/PDF/?uri=CELEX:32016R0679
4 UK Government (2018). "Section 9, Data Protection Act 2018". http://www.legislation.gov.uk/ukpga/2018/12/section/9/enacted
5 Federal Trade Commission (1998). "The Children's Online Privacy Protection Act 1998". https://www.ftc.gov/enforcement/rules/rulemaking-regulatory-reform-proceedings/childrens-online-privacy-protection-rule

the term "pornography" to describe sexual imagery featuring children.[6,7] The term "pornography" refers to recordings of adults engaging in consensual sexual acts, distributed for sexual pleasure. However, as defined in law, children cannot consent to sexual acts and, by extension, are not willing participants in the production of sexual imagery. They are victims of criminal acts. Therefore, applying the term "revenge pornography" to the material of minors can detract from the possible severity of these crimes.

However, an exception can also be taken with the term "revenge pornography" in general, given that most acts described as such have their justification in a vengeful or pornographic element.

Early Perspectives on Revenge Pornography

The early recognition of revenge pornography as a term related to websites that provided the facilities for slighted partners to post intimate materials of people with whom they had been in a relationship. These "revenge" websites, such as IsAnyoneUp, IsAnyBodyDown or UGotPosted marketed themselves as pornography sites with "user-driven content". However, much content posted on these sites involved intimate images of individuals where contributors would link to people's social media profiles. While these images were frequently either nude or images of victims engaged in sex acts, the motivation for the websites was financial for the site owners. Before being shut down by the FBI (as a result of an investigation that many of the images were obtained by hacking victim's email accounts, rather than having them donated by "anonymous contributors"), it was estimated that IsAnyoneUp was generating $13,000 per month[8] from advertising revenue. IsAnyBodyDown offered a "takedown service"[9] for victims where, in exchange for payment, the website would offer, then fail, to take down images of them shared without consent. They also provided prizes for users who could identify, by providing links to social media pages, anonymous images on their site.

A similar "business model" was operated by the owner of UGotPosted,[10] Kevin Bollaert, who ran a parallel website, ChangeMyReputation, where those who had seen their images (non-consensually) posted on UGotPosted were told the posts

6 Kettleborough, D. (2015). "What's wrong with "child pornography"? The impact of terminology" [Weblog post]. http://wp.me/p2RS15-9f
7 Interpol (n.d.). "Appropriate Terminology". https://www.interpol.int/en/Crimes/Crimes-against-children/Appropriate-terminology
8 Gold, D. (2011). "The Man Who Makes Money Publishing Your Nude Pics". *The Awl.* https://www.theawl.com/2011/11/the-man-who-makes-money-publishing-your-nude-pics/
9 FTC (2015). "Website Operator Banned from the 'Revenge Porn' Business After FTC Charges He Unfairly Posted Nude Photos". https://www.ftc.gov/news-events/press-releases/2015/01/website-operator-banned-revenge-porn-business-after-ftc-charges
10 Vaas, L. (2015). "Revenge-Porn Website Operator Kevin Bollaert guilty of identity theft and extortion". *Sophos.* https://nakedsecurity.sophos.com/2015/02/04/revenge-porn-website-operator-kevin-bollaert-guilty-of-identity-theft-and-extortion/

could be removed if they paid a fee. Mr Bollaert was eventually arrested and charged, and while his defence was that he could not be held responsible for site users posting non-consensual content, he was ultimately found guilty of 27 counts, including conspiracy, identity theft and extortion, and sentenced to 18 years in prison.

A more recent mass "revenge pornography" incident centred around Marines United,[11] a movement among US Marines (and other servicemen) to distribute intimate images of ex-partners across shared online drives and social media sites. Exposed by former marine and journalist Thomas Brennan, it was estimated that there were, in total, approximately 30,000 members across 168 sites and shared drives, with in excess of 131,000 images shared.

In response to the breaking story, the US Department of Defense issued a statement:[12]

Lack of respect for the dignity and humanity of fellow members of the Department of Defense is unacceptable and harmful to the unit cohesion necessary to battlefield victory. We will not excuse or tolerate such behavior if we are to uphold our values and maintain our ability to defeat the enemy on the battlefield.

A Naval Criminal Investigative Service identified 89 persons of interest – 22 civilians and 67 active-duty marines, most of whom have now been disciplined to varying degrees within military courts.

However, since breaking the story, Brennan has been subject to online abuse including demands he is waterboarded and one posted offering $500 for an intimate image of his daughter.[13] While the Department of Defense seemed clear on the values needed to be upheld by their staff, it would seem that this might not necessarily have been reflected in their behaviour. Indeed, since the statement and news story broke there were subsequent reports of secondary groups and new shared drives emerging to provide similar services.[14] In the reporting[15] of the first

11 Brennan, T. (2017). "Hundreds of Marines investigated for sharing photos of Naked Colleagues". *Reveal.* https://www.revealnews.org/blog/hundreds-of-marines-investigated-for-sharing-photos-of-naked-colleagues/

12 US Department of Defense (2017). "Statement by Secretary of Defense Jim Mattis on Purported Actions Detrimental to Good Order and Discipline". https://dod.defense.gov/News/News-Releases/News-Release-View/Article/1109833/statement-by-secretary-of-defense-jim-mattis-on-purported-actions-detrimental-t/

13 CBS News (2017). "Marines Being Investigated Over Salacious Photo Sharing of Women Service Members". https://www.cbsnews.com/news/marines-being-investigated-over-salacious-photo-sharing-of-women-service-members/?ftag=CNM-00-10aab7e&linkId=35134260

14 LaPorta, J., and Lavery, R. (2017). "The Marine Nude-Photo Scandal Is Growing and Adding New Victims". *The Daily Beast.* https://www.thedailybeast.com/the-marine-nude-photo-scandal-is-growing-and-adding-new-victims

15 Barnes, L. (2017). "First Man Court-Martialed Over 'Marines United' Scandal Where Servicemen Shared Explicit Photos of Female Colleagues on Facebook page". *The Daily Mail.*

court martial of a marine related to behaviour on the sites, the public comments following the article were fairly typical in victim blaming, suggesting once more that the fault lay with the taker and sender of the image, rather than the person who non-consensually distributed it further. One poster went further, suggesting this is what happens when you include women in "masculine" professions such as the marines.

When UK actress Kira Martin spoke about her experiences after her ex-boyfriend shared topless images of her on social media and in a group chat, the website UniLad ran the story and posted it on their Facebook page.[16] Among the responses were, again, plenty that blamed the victim, even though some of the posters were at pains to point out they weren't victim blaming, before blaming the victim.

Drawing from the literature, for example,[17] there are a diverse set of motivations for posting "revenge pornography", and even more justifications for doing so. While there is much discussion around "revenge" being the primary motivation for the poster (i.e. a relationship has broken down and therefore the "injured party" gets "revenge" by sharing intimate images), even with the small number of examples above, financial gain seems to be a significant driver for these sorts of behaviours. While those posting these images may try to justify the distribution as revenge, to share intimate images of ex-partners just because they have had the audacity to decide they no longer wish to be in a relationship with them seems utterly disproportionate and not revenge, but abuse. The recent Shattering Lives report,[18] which spoke to both victims of image-based and stakeholders in this area, makes a very clear argument that the term is a myth, and those sharing images non-consensually are not doing so for revenge. Instead, the authors state:

> The reality is that image-based sexual abuse is motivated by control, as well as misogyny, men's entitlement and "laddish" attitudes.

While this is certainly true in a lot of cases, as an exploration of the Revenge Porn Helpline cases will illustrate, not all image-based abuse is male on female. The power these images grant the abuser over the victim should be acknowledged. If one is in possession of intimate images of another, it is understandable that they will not wish for those images to be shared. Therefore, the threat of sharing these images allows control of the victim to either coerce them into behaviours they would be unwilling to do without this coercion (for example, sending further

http://www.dailymail.co.uk/news/article-4685694/First-man-court-martialed-Marines-United-scandal.html
16 https://www.facebook.com/uniladmag/videos/3035119496511089/
17 McGlynn, C., and Rackley, E. (2017). "Image-based sexual abuse". *Oxford Journal of Legal Studies, 37*(1), 534–561.
18 McGlynn, C., Rackley, E., & Johnson, K. (2019). "Shattering lives and myths: A Report on Image-Based Sexual Abuse". *Durham University.* https://www.dur.ac.uk/resources/law/ShatteringLivesandMythsFINALJuly2019.pdf

images) or to blackmail or further harass the victim. It is, perhaps, more powerful to hold the images with the threat of sharing, rather than actually sharing them due to the control the abuser can hold over the victim. This is something we will be returning to later in this discussion. However, the links to more serious crimes, such as sexual assault and sexual harassment as a result of being in possession of images or videos, is still not something that is frequently recognised.[16]

While the origination of images tends to involve an ex-partner circulating, or threatening to circulate, intimate images which were only consented for private use, this is not the only means by which images are obtained. In the case of IsAnyoneUp's owner Hunter Moore, his final prosecution was not as a result of sharing non-consensual images or copyright infringement, but by hacking and theft.[19]

In terms of the location of images and other media, this can also be diverse. While pornographic sites and more "specialist" revenge/user-driven content pornography sites are viewed as the main route to dissemination,[20] this is not always the case. A study conducted by McAfee in 2013 found that over 50% of adults distributed sexually explicit images via a mobile device.[18] Social media is also used frequently to distribute this kind of material, and while most mainstream social media sites have strict takedown policies, one thing to note with these different approaches is that, in the case of "specialist" sites and social media, there is an opportunity for others to comment, usually misogynistically and, in some cases, with threatening and violent comments.[13.]

As an aside, it is worth exploring a couple of the policy statements around revenge pornography takedowns. For Pornhub the statement on takedowns[21] is short and lacking in detail and, interestingly, relates to the copyright ownership of media, rather than consent or harm:

> Pornhub takes all content removal requests seriously. Should you be a victim of revenge porn, blackmailing or intimidation because of a video or photo of yourself on our sites that you did not authorize, please complete the form below and we will remove the content expeditiously.
>
> For all other content removal requests related to copyright infringement, please contact copyright@pornhub.com or use the DMCA takedown request form on /information#dmca.

---

19 McGlynn, C., and Rackley, E. (2017). "Image-based sexual abuse". *Oxford Journal of Legal Studies, 37*(1), 534–561.
20 Hall, M., and Hearn, J. (2018) "Revenge Pornography: Gender, Sexuality and Motivations". Routledge.
21 Pornhub (2018). "Copyright Removal Request". https://www.pornhub.com/content-removal

For Facebook, a leak of their internal policy documents in 2017[22] detailed what they use internally to decide whether a piece of media is "revenge pornography" and therefore whether it should be taken down:

High-level: Revenge porn is sharing nude/near-nude photos of someone publicly or to people that they didn't want to see them in order to shame or embarrass them.

Abuse standards:
6. Attempting to exploit intimate images by any of the following:
Sharing images as "revenge porn" if it fulfils all three conditions:
Image produced in a private setting
Person in image is nude, near nude or sexually active
Lack of consent confirmed by:
Vengeful content (e.g. caption, comment or page title), OR
Independent sources (e.g. media coverage or LE record)

While the role of service providers will be explored in far more detail in later chapters, these two notices raise important points early in these discussions. First, Pornhub focuses entirely on the copyright of the image, rather than exploring issues of consent or harm. Prior to the emergence of "revenge pornography" specific legislation, copyright was usually viewed as the best way to tackle non-consensual sharing.[23] Given that the majority of these images and videos are "self-generated", copyright law (for example, the US Digital Millennium Copyright Act 1998[24]) states the copyright is retained by the taker of the image (and therefore the subject of the image too). While this is a useful legal solution to preventing images being shared, especially on public platforms, it fails to deal with the more serious issues arising from the non-consensual sharing of images, such as harm or further abuse.

Consent, which is raised in the Facebook policy, is also an interesting challenge as it is argued that if consent can be used for sharing an image, then consent cannot be withdrawn for further sharing.[25] However, this is a somewhat facile argument, one cannot "pass on" consent to other circumstances. If one is to provide consent for one act, it does not automatically fall that this consent can now be

22 Hopkins, N. (2017). "Revealed: Facebook's Internal Rulebook on sex, terrorism and violence". *The Guardian*. https://www.theguardian.com/news/2017/may/21/revealed-facebook-internal-rulebook-sex-terrorism-violence
23 Levendowski, A. (2014). "Using Copyright to Combat Revenge Porn". New York University School of Law. Available at: http://jipel.law.nyu.edu/wp-content/uploads/2015/05/NYU_JIPEL_Vol-3-No-2_6_Levendowski_RevengePorn.pdf
24 US Copyright Office (1998). "The Digital Millennium Copyright Act 1998". https://www.copyright.gov/legislation/dmca.pdf
25 Citron, D., and Franks, M. (2014). "Criminalizing revenge porn". *Wake Forest Law Review*, 49, 345–391. Available at: http://digitalcommons.law.umaryland.edu/cgi/viewcontent.cgi?article=2424&context=fac_pubs

used for any further act. To take an example of consensual sexual intercourse, one does not consent once and from that point on it is not necessary to be sought – it must be requested in every instance. Just because someone has consented to sharing an image of themselves with a single third party, it does not mean they further consent to that third party sharing the image with anyone they wish.

This is why the Facebook policy definition on consent is somewhat concerning. In their policy statement, they say lack of consent is obtained as a result of associated posting (for example, abusive comments alongside the image) or confirmed by other sources (for example, if the police confirm that consent was not obtained). It would seem, from our interpretation of this statement, that confirmation of lack of consent from the victim is not sufficient, they need to provide corroborating evidence of lack of consent.

Impact on Victims

Discussing the impact on victims with staff from the Revenge Porn Helpline (explored in more detail below) showed that the effect of the non-consensual sharing of images can be severe, impacting on mental health, social life and work life. The impact can also remain long term – this is not an act that can easily be laughed off. Discussions with helpline staff reflected a number of issues that are shown in the literature, which categorises both psychological and "lifestyle impact". In the Shattering Lives report,[26] the authors describe a "social rupture" that occurs when someone becomes a victim of image-based abuse. This rupture causes changes to all aspects of their lives – it is not something that can be shrugged off or ignored.

Citron and Franks[18] develop further categorisation on psychological impact, raising concerns around anxiety that can possibly lead to suicidal tendencies. The harm that can arise from the non-consensual sharing of images cannot be underestimated. Moreover, there can be impacts such as concerns for personal safety, body image anxieties, long-term trust issues and, as illustrated in the quotes above, simply the anxiety of not knowing where images have been posted, whether new images will emerge or how many people have seen them.

There is impact of lifestyle, for example, issues around education and employment. In an example given below from the Revenge Porn Helpline, a victim of a serious non-consensual disclosure was suspended from her job. The helpline makes it clear on their website this is something that has occurred for many clients.[27] Obviously, the impact on employment can also have a knock-on effect on finances. Equally, financial risk can rise from being extorted by an ex-partner or third party as a result of the images being online (indeed, this was the business model for UGotPosted and IsAnyoneUp).

---

26 Ibid.
27 Revenge Porn Helpline (n.d.) "About Intimate Image Abuse". https://revengepornhelpli ne.org.uk/information-and-advice/about-intimate-image-abuse/

There is also the risk of harassment, particularly if, as is the case with a lot of non-consensual sharing, the poster also included personal details of the victim. While the platforms themselves, along with social media, provide routes for others to harass the victims, there is a very real risk that they will also be subject to physical harassment as a result of these posts. As a result of non-consensual sharing, many victims disclose that they have changed phone numbers, social media profiles and even moved house.[18] Furthermore, the "posting revealing photos of non-consenting others along with identifying information potentially leads to humiliation and embarrassment and could increase the potential for online and 'real-life' harassment".[28] It is also known, as a result of shame and embarrassment, that many victims will withdraw themselves from friends and family[29] at a time when, as disclosed by victims, having support around them can be critically important to moving on and addressing mental health issues.

In further developing an argument about the appropriateness of the term, the following specific case is drawn from the Revenge Porn Helpline. This case is illustrative because it highlights not just the impact of the act on the victim, but also how victims can be let down by those supposedly tasked with protecting them.

In this case, the helpline was approached by someone who said that they worked as a teacher and it had been disclosed to her that pupils had discovered an intimate video of her published on Pornhub. The video had been on the site for three years before she was made aware and it was taken when she was 15 years old. The helpline requested a takedown from Pornhub, based not only upon the fact that it was posted without consent but also because the subject in the video was a minor and the content was therefore illegal. Thankfully, Pornhub took the video down immediately. However, the harm to the victim was exacerbated because she was suspended by her employer for misconduct. Furthermore, when approaching the police with the name of the poster of the video (an ex-partner), no action was taken against him, even though he was posting an indecent video of a minor.

Within this case, victimisation is not merely arising from the individual who posted the image, but through failures of other stakeholders in the welfare of the victim. For example, the employer, who should have had a duty of care for the victim (who had done nothing wrong other than produce an explicit video, something many of the population have done) – the victim did not share the video more widely or post it on a pornography site, and she did not promote the video such that pupils at her school were exposed to it. There is little justification for her employer to suspend her, other than for reputation management of the

28 Stroud, S. R. (2014). "The dark side of the online self: A pragmatist critique of the growing plague of revenge porn". *Journal of Mass media Ethics, 29*(3), 168–183.
29 Walker, K., and Sleath, E. (2017). "A systematic review of the current knowledge regarding revenge pornography and non-consensual sharing of sexually explicit media". *Aggression and Violent Behaviour, 36,* 9–24.

organisation – they did not wish to deal with the fact that one of their staff had become a victim of the non-consensual sharing of a video of her and preferred to just say that the victim no longer worked at their establishment when local concerns were raised. This is not an unusual response from an employer or other stakeholder with a duty of care (for example, in the event of students at a university), and It is something explored in more detail later in this chapter.

Moreover, the victim was clearly let down by law enforcement given her ex-partner had non-consensually shared illegal content of the victim, this should be a clear cause for intervention. While this case arose after the royal assent and commencement of the Criminal Justice and Courts Act (2015), the crime was enacted before this was on the statute books. However, the nature of the material posted clearly fits with the Protection of Children Act 1978, section 1, and it is therefore concerning that law enforcement did not even speak with the poster of the video.

Therefore, the term *revenge pornography* is not helpful. If we take definitions of each word in turn:

> Revenge:[30] the action of hurting or harming someone in return for an injury or wrong suffered at their hands.

By using the term "revenge" to talk about these crimes, we are, in essence, providing some reason or excuse for this behaviour. The perpetrator is taking revenge on the victim, for a slight the victim has performed on them. In the case of non-consensually sharing intimate images of an ex-partner, this is not revenge, this is abuse.

> Pornography:[31] printed or visual material containing the explicit description or display of sexual organs or activity, intended to stimulate sexual excitement.

In the second part of the definition, while one might argue that self-produced sexually explicit material might have been produced to stimulate sexual excitement, the intention of the individual sharing the images/materials in a non-consensual way is not for sexual excitement, it is to harm, to embarrass, to shame and to hurt the subject of the images. While sexual excitement might arise for those viewing these images, it is not the intention of the poster.

Through this exploration of cases and responses, it can be seen that these behaviours rarely have justification in revenge. Moreover, by using the term "revenge pornography", it, in some way, legitimises the behaviour of the abuser and lessens the harm to the victim. By calling it revenge, one implies there is fault on both sides, rather than unwarranted abuse. There is a need to start referring

---

30 https://en.oxforddictionaries.com/definition/revenge
31 https://en.oxforddictionaries.com/definition/pornography

to "revenge pornography" for what it is – image-based abuse as part of domestic abuse, exploitation, coercion and harassment.

Nevertheless, for the sake of discussion, and to align with popular discourse, the term "revenge pornography" will be used when discussing themes, behaviours and legislation around the non-consensual sharing of intimate images and videos. However, the problematic terminology will be returned to later in this text.

The remainder of this chapter, as with the previous chapter, draws from empirical experiences in the field, this time making extensive use of both interviews with, and case analysis of, the Revenge Porn Helpline. This develops the issues raised around the context of revenge pornography drawn from literature, media reporting and policy analysis, and is used in order to explore the environment in which the new legislation was developed. One of the central theses in this text is that we need to understand grassroots behaviours in order to result in more effective legislation, and legislation that looks across the whole vista, rather than focusing upon, for example, the act. The case of teen sexting has already established that a focus on the act of self-generation and non-consensual sharing, rather than understanding the broad environment in which these acts occur, results in legislative intervention that can revictimise a victim and treat them as an offender. While this is less likely with the adult non-consensual sharing of images, except in the event of the images being above thresholds for obscenity, if one, again, focuses on the act, and tries to legislate to prevent the act from occurring, one will only ever achieve vaguely adequate, rather than landmark, legislation. In working with the Revenge Porn Helpline, the empirical analysis can present a more complete vista, and, as such, better understand where victims need protection and how that might be achieved.

A *Typical* Revenge Pornography Scenario

Drawing from interviews with Revenge Porn Helpline staff between 2017 and 2020, and detailed exploration of their case book over the same period, what is clear is that there is no "typical" revenge pornography scenario or client. While they deal with many cases one might consider to be the "usual" in terms of modus operandi (i.e. an ex-partner non-consensually shares intimate images of the victim either onto a public online space or to targeted private individuals), they deal with as many that do not fit into this category.

Their client age is wide-ranging, from minors to those far older. One worker on the helpline said that the majority of clients fell between the ages of 20 and 50; however, they have also dealt with younger (in the case of minors, they would generally be dealing with their parents as well as the victim themselves) and those far older. And while the majority of clients they work with are female, a significant minority (around 25%) are male. There were general differences in the type of abuse depending on the gender of clients, but they saw many different types of exploitation for both genders.

There were also cultural differences discussed. For example, depending on culture, the "threshold" for shame differed. For example, they had dealt with a number of cases within Asian communities, particularly around arranged marriages, where the images shared (or threatened to be shared) were no worse than underwear or cleavage pictures. However, the impact on the victim, and abuse from within the community, was as bad as that suffered by those who shared far more intimate images within a different culture. While, to those working on the helpline, and certainly from our perspective working in the field for a number of years, these images were nowhere near as "indecent" as the sort of thing one might find on certain tabloid news websites, the impact upon the victims could be severe, with "honour"-based abuse becoming an issue. Clients had been shamed within their community and even abused by their own family as a result of a partner posting these images.

This again raises a challenge against legislation around intention to harm and victim upset, as has already been discussed in Chapter 2. If the victim is upset, abused or harmed as a result of the images being shared, surely this is a more significant driver for prosecution than the categorisation of image.

The helpline also raised different issues in terms of sexuality. They dealt with a lot of calls from the LGBTQ community (around 25% of inquiries) and again impact would vary depending upon victim profile and culture. However, one recurring theme centred around people being "outed" in Asian communities through the sharing of images, and the shame that arose as a result of these actions.

While the service is referred to as a "helpline", they actually provide three main routes of inquiry: a phone number, an email inquiry and an anonymous reporting form. Obviously, the anonymous reporting does limit what the helpline can do in response, but it is a valuable part of the service for those inquirers who are too ashamed to risk being identified. Overall, the helpline is contacted via email (approximately 60%) more than phone calls (around 35%) and the anonymous tool (5%). However, there were similarities when it came to why the client was contacting the service.

In general, people contacted the service because they felt they had nowhere else to turn. They have exhausted options themselves, which may have included pleading with the offender, contacting service and platform providers and talking to friends and family. One key trigger for them contacting the service was after the images had been shared. While they felt that they could deal with the issues when an abuser was threatening to share images, once they had moved from private threat to the public online space, the victim felt that they were no longer in control and had no idea how to manage the disclosure. They would turn to the helpline in order to try to get the images removed because their own efforts were often in vain. On rare occasions, the helpline was told that the victim had been advised by the police to contact them because they would be more proactive than law enforcement.

A lot of contact begins with the client saying that this was not something they had ever done before but they needed help because things had got out of control, they were being abused or they had no idea how to deal with the spreading of images. There are a number of similar responses and comments from clients on first contact regarding the production of the images and initial sharing. A lot of them talked about how they had been *nagged* into sending images. Perhaps a better word for the description of behaviours associated with this nagging (i.e. comments like "if you loved me you'd do this", "don't you trust me" or more positive comments about how attractive they were and the offender would love to see images/videos) would be *coercion*. This shows parallels with earlier discussions around teen sexting and the pressure received by a lot of victims which resulted in them producing an image just to make the pressure stop. A lot of clients talked about how they felt it was difficult to say no with persistent, albeit "friendly", requests, and some admitted to it being flattering to receive these requests and perhaps nice to have attention from someone who they believed felt they were attractive.

However, some clients also talked about more aggressive forms of coercion, such as being pressured into generating images as a component in an abusive relationship or forced intramarital activity. In these cases, due to the repercussions if they were to say no, they felt that this was not an option for them. And, of course, once abusive partners had images that were "self-generated", they then used them to coerce the victim into other sexual acts or further production of media. In further cases, content might have been captured or filmed without the knowledge of the victim and, again, raises serious challenges to privacy considerations as well as consent.

Other clients talked about how they had not shared images with a partner but had them stolen from a device. This was generally either as a result of the partner (or ex-partner) being able to access the device or storage through knowing the password and other authentications methods, or the images were taken from devices without any form of protection.

In some of the instances, the already weak argument of consent to share falls even further. If the victim did not consent to the acquisition of the image in the first place, there is no question that "transferred consent" could be argued. However, many of the other victims who had sent partners or abusers images as a result of requests or pressure were often ready to blame themselves for this very reason. Many felt that once the image was in the abuser's possession, they were entitled to do what they wished with it, regardless of promises not to share further or that consent had been sought. A lot of victims blamed themselves for the images being shared or posted onto public platforms – they should not have taken the images in the first place, they should not have sent them or they have no right over the images once they have been shared.

A lot of victims were not aware of sexual culture online, many would start the conversation with "I've never done anything like this before", and many say they have never looked at pornography and certainly don't understand the volume of content there is, the frequency of this sort of abuse or how they might respond to non-consensual sharing.

One thing that also came across very strongly from discussions with the helpline staff and the exploration of the cases was the amount of time a victim was subject not to the sharing of an image but the threat to share. For example, the offender would have received images from the victim, then used the threat to share the images as a means to coerce or exploit the victim further, therefore, unless they sent more images or engaged in sexual acts with the offender, the images would be posted online or shared with people known to the victim (a lot of the time this would be employers or family). In many ways, the threat of sharing is more powerful than the act of sharing itself – once the image has been shared, the offender has reduced their power over the victim because the impact of sharing has been achieved. However, this is not always the case, particularly when a campaign of abuse is conducted by the offender, as the image can be shared multiple times with multiple targets. The helpline talked about repeat callers who had been subjected to sharing and re-sharing of images – in one case, the offender shared the images with every new employer the victim had. In these cases, a repeated revictimisation occurs – every time the images are viewed by a new third party, the harm and shame are repeated as the victim experiences these harms again.

Moreover, there is another seriously distressing impact around not knowing who has seen the images and where they have ended up. And while the images may have been shared once, unless the offender is tackled about their behaviour, there is no guarantee that the images will not be shared again. The uncertainty is another aspect of harm that is lacking in a lot of the discussion and literature around revenge pornography. With the focus on the non-consensual act of sharing, there is an assumption these are one-off offences. In reality, victims can be subject to abuse many times, and from many different perspectives.

The online dissemination of images, and the lack of control of the image once it is either shared with multiple parties or posted in a public online space, means that the audience for viewing the image is entirely unknown. With digital images sharing once does not prevent further sharing unless the offender is challenged on their behaviour and taken to task with what they have done. There is a crucial need for legislation to protect victims because, in a lot of instances, offenders feel they can do what they like with no challenge to their behaviour. Once images are in their possession, there is a persistent threat to the victim, and once images have been shared once, there is no guarantee that the sharing of images can be controlled further or who ends up seeing them.

Types of Behaviour

In terms of the types of behaviour associated with revenge pornography "offences",[32] again, there was a broad range described by the helpline and within

---

32 The quotes for the word "offence" are deliberate – while some of the behaviours described would fall under the 2015 legislation, and some would fit into other laws, as we develop our arguments in this book, one of the pivotal points is that there is no legislation that protects from all acts at the present time and some behaviours would not be considered offences in the legislative framework we currently have.

the cases. In terms of the destination of images, there were two primary routes of dissemination – either public websites or targeted groups.

For public dissemination, social media was sometimes used, however, this was not a popular choice given the increased and improving awareness of revenge pornography by these platforms and their proactivity in takedowns. In a lot of cases, in the experience of the helpline practitioners, takedowns would not require their intervention, as victims proactive in their own reporting to these providers would often see images removed. Far more popular targets were the large pornography providers, such as Pornhub and XHamster. However, even these sites were more proactive than they used to be (see the above discussion around Pornhub's takedown policy) and while there would usually be challenged over copyright, takedowns would still occur (XHamster also operates a takedown "policy" based upon the Digital Millennium Copyright Act 1998, the copyright legislation within their jurisdiction[33]). The US Digital Millennium Copyright Act has also been successfully applied in a lot of cases of non-consensual posting due to the subject and taker (usually the same person) of the image retaining copyright over it. The act makes specific provision (section 230) for service providers to be held responsible for breaches of copyright if they do not meet certain conditions. One of these conditions is they must comply with takedown requests. If they respond to takedown requests, they can be seen to be compliant with the act, if they do not, they could be considered liable for copyright infringement, with potential fines of $150,000 per image.[34]

Therefore, a lot of images ended up in the less well-regulated end of public pornographic websites, which were often hosted in eastern European or Asian countries where less stringent copyright or victim protection legislation would be in operation. This, of course, also presented a challenge for the helpline in that they had no contacts with these sites and often struggled to get takedowns enacted.

It was also observed that there are differences in the public platforms chosen for younger victims, particularly those who might look underaged. There is a clear pattern here for material that would be illegal as indecent images of minors, or those that looked like they were, staying away from "mainstream" sites in general, and appearing on less well-regulated sites such as Anon.IB and 4chan. They would also appear on specialist sites (i.e. for specific ethnic groups) which were also less stringent in their moderation or hosted in counties where copyright or content control legislation was less well controlled. Anon.IB was taken down in 2018 by Dutch police,[35] but this was not as a result of hosting "revenge por-

---

33 XHamster (2018). "DMCA Notice & Takedown Policy and Procedures". https://pt.xhamster.com/info/dmca (Accessed October 2018).
34 Harvard University Digital Millennium Copyright Act (n.d.). "Annual Copyright Disclosure". https://dmca.harvard.edu/pages/annual-copyright-disclosure
35 Ng, A. (2018). "Massive Revenge Porn Site Anon-IB Shut Down by Dutch police". *cnet.* https://www.cnet.com/news/massive-revenge-porn-website-anon-ib-shut-down-by-dutch-police/

nography" images, but because, similar to the IsAnybodyUp takedown, the site owners were obtaining images by hacking into victim's personal file stores and distributing images obtained from there, rather than because other posters were sharing images on the site.

For targeted groups, generally platforms offering "group chat" and similar features were used, so apps such as WhatsApp tended to be popular. There is nothing specific to these platforms that make them "better" for revenge pornography, they are just popular communication platforms that allow the distribution of different types of media, so they suit the purposes of the offender. Furthermore, other approaches such as email might be used if the offender wishes to target specific individuals, such as employers. They will either be sent the images via email or pointed to links where the images are hosted.

Motivations for sharing are also wide-ranging. While many could be argued (poorly) by offenders as "revenge", given they are trying to harm an ex-partner, many cases fall far outside of that sort of motivation. For some, there is clearly a financial incentive (see below), for others, this is part of a wider campaign of domestic abuse. There are many cases where partners have used images to coerce victims into more producing more sexual content or engaging in sexual acts. In these cases, control and the power afforded by being in possession of images is the pivotal motivation. In some cases, the victim is approached by a stranger who has managed to track them down as a result of being on a "revenge pornography" website (many sites encourage posts to link intimate images to social media profiles of victims so they can be traced easily by those wishing to harass) and will use the images to try to extort money, obtain further images or even sexual contact with the victim. Finally, the helpline deals with a lot of victims who end-up dealing with the fallout from "banter" – from a partner sharing an image with a group of friends, to the more public sharing on pages such as those like Marines United (sometimes referred to as "Blockrat" style posts). While the intention in those cases by offenders might be more to show "what a lad" they are to friends and peers, the harm to victims is still significant. However, there are challenges to these sorts of cases where offenders claim there was no intention to harm but to impress their peers.

The helpline has, since its establishment, seen far more contact from (predominantly) males who have become victims of extortion as a result of engaging in sexual conduct with a stranger on a website. This is probably one of the areas the helpline deals with where more victims are male than female. This is sometimes, unhelpfully, referred to as *sextortion*, whereas a better term would be online sexual coercion and extortion. An example and common scenario would be a victim receiving a connection or friend request via social media where, once the request is accepted, the offender (generally using a fake profile) will groom the victim into engaging in sexual acts via a webcam through popular platforms such as Facebook video chat, Skype or Facetime. The act will then be captured and the offender will start to make threats to share the images (usually on platforms such as YouTube) unless the victim pays them a fee. In some cases, offenders (who seem to be part of organised groups) will create fake YouTube posts to share with the victim to put more pressure on them for payment (helpline practitioners say payment generally ranges from about £500 to £5000). If payment is made, the extortion will generally increase with further demands for funds. For this reason, helpline advice is usually to not make payments, as this is no guarantee of removal or deletion. As discussed above, the release of a digital asset does not prevent it from being subsequently shared.

However, there are new types of behaviour and types of abuse arising all of the time, and this is highlighted by some recent cases raised by practitioners. Each case was new to the helpline in terms of operation, and while there were links into similar revenge pornography scenarios, the cases show the breadth of abuse the helpline deals with and the complexity in providing advice to victims. The cases are described briefly below to illustrate the diversity of abuse.

Case 1: A victim contacted the helpline to say that their partner had lost their mobile phone and it was recovered by a stranger who could access the device. The stranger then contacted the victim, claiming to be her partner (she was not aware at that stage he had lost his phone) and asking for more intimate content. The victim, assuming she was conversing with her partner, sent the images that were then posted on a revenge pornography website.

Case 2: A male victim contacted the helpline to say he was being extorted for money as a result of a strange event that occurred while walking his dog. He noticed a white van parked in the woods where he was walking his dog and was met by a gentleman who asked him if he wanted to look at videos of his wife he had on a mobile device in the van. The gentleman told him to "make use" of the video if he wanted while he went for a walk. Upon returning to the van the victim was told by the gentleman that he had been recorded masturbating on a hidden camera in the van and unless he paid a fee, he would share the video online.

Case 3: One young victim's mother contacted the helpline because the victim had been notified that there was a video of her, aged 12, hosted on a well-known pornography site. The video had been on the site for three years and was only taken down once it was pointed out that the video was of a child. Since being made aware of the video, and the duration of its exposure, the victim had become depressed and suicidal, experiencing repeated revictimisation as a result of the viewing of the video.

This diversity was not unique, the case book also contains examples of voyeurism (a dispute between neighbours where one party filmed the others engaged in a sexual act and threatened to share the video); "revenge" by new spouses accessing their partner's online storage or other devices to discover images of ex-partners and then sharing these with friends and family; and employers using images to coerce employees.

Response from Stakeholders

One thing that was also explored with the helpline and in their cases was the support victims received from other stakeholders. In an initial exploration, what became clear was victim frustration, while sometimes levelled at service providers, it was mainly centred around their treatment when reporting incidents to law enforcement.

For platform providers, it is clear that responses to both victims and the helpline are variable. While the larger social media providers were generally responsive to the helpline, the experiences victims had prior to contacting the helpline was sometimes less successful. However, the helpline also said that some social media companies seemed to show more compassion for victims than others, with some only responding to queries around their legal responsibilities, rather than the harm to the individual. As already discussed, the response from pornography providers seemed to be very legal in focus – they would take down illegal content (i.e. indecent images of children) quickly, but anything else could only be challenged via copyright protection legislation. If copyright was not held by the victim, there was no clear route for takedown. Consent seemed to be less of a concern (one might imagine because there is no legal responsibility for the provider in terms of consent or harm to the victim).

For the smaller providers, and image board hosts, the responses can be more variable, although some will be cooperative as a result of copyright infringement. However, those hosted outside of any jurisdiction where copyright legislation is effective are generally far less cooperative.

However, most frustration, for both victims and helpline practitioners, was in the response of law enforcement to revenge pornography reports. It was observed that the biggest barrier to both the protection of victims and the prosecution of offenders lay with the response of the police when crimes were reported. Many different responses from law enforcement were reported by clients of the helpline; however, the vast majority of them were negative. A lot of responses centred on the lack of understanding or empathy by officers, and a lack of acknowledgement that a criminal offence may have been committed. In a number of client experiences, they were made to feel, by police they had reported the crime to, that this sort of crime was not worthy of their time or a belief that the offender had done nothing wrong. In many instances, this reflected the wider cultural view that the victim was at fault for sharing images in the first place, with one client being told "well you shouldn't have taken the pictures, then he wouldn't have been able to share them". There seemed, from an exploration of cases the helpline has dealt with, that a lot of the time the police response was ignorant of the criminal activity around revenge pornography or even the legislation. In another case, a victim reported her ex-partner non-consensually sharing images of her online and the response from the police officer was that he'd done nothing wrong. They only admitted their mistake when the victim printed off the legislation (section 33 of the Serious Crime and Courts Act 2015) and showed it to the officer. More seriously in one case, a victim reported that her ex-partner (a serving police officer) was given time to remove images from his laptop before he was subject to a search so that he could claim he was not in possession of images that had been shared online.

One area of abuse where the helpline and clients did find the police more responsive and engaged was around issues where extortion became a part of the case. With extortion related incidents, the helpline said that had a good relationship with the Kidnap and Extortion Unit within the National Crime Agency, and they have seen many active, coordinated responses from this unit when the helpline referred cases to them. They have provided the helpline with guidance on how to advise clients to report crimes to the unit and clear workflows in how they will respond. The unit is also proactive at tracking down suspicious accounts on social media platforms, particularly with multiple accounts coming from the same location.

There are some interesting things to reflect upon here. First, there is a clear route for the helpline to work at a national level on extortion cases. The law enforcement professionals they are dealing with will be specialist in the area and will have received training around the criminal activity associated with these incidents. And as such, there are clear routes for responses and dealing with victims. This is quite clearly not the case with crimes that would fit more broadly into revenge pornography scenarios – there is no national coordination centre for revenge pornography crimes, and therefore, victims and the helpline have to liaise with regional forces. Given there is no national priority around revenge pornography, there is little training available to forces (research by Emma Bond in 2018[36] showed that only 5% of police officers surveyed had received any training around image-based abuse) and the response from law enforcement can literally hinge on the views and opinions of an individual within a force.

Parallels and Differences

This chapter has explored the phenomenon of revenge pornography and seen that, in some ways, there are similarities with teen sexting, and in other ways, there are large differences. Perhaps the most significant difference, when considered from a legal perspective, is that there should be far less ambiguity around the legality of the conduct of the victim in these cases. While images are "self-generated", the vast majority of these images would not fall foul of obscenity laws. There is legislation developed to protect victims of the non-consensual sharing of images, and it could be applied in a lot of cases to achieve this protection.

However, for a number of reasons, this is clearly not happening. While the next two chapters will explore the legislation and the lived experience in the courts, for both teen sexting and revenge pornography, we draw this chapter to

---

36 Bond, E., & Tyrrell, K. (2018). "Understanding revenge pornography: A National survey of police officers and staff in England and Wales". *Journal of Interpersonal Violence*. doi: 10.1177/ 0886260518760011

a close by considering the central commonality between these phenomena before considering whether the legislation is adequate in addressing this.

As can be seen from disclosures by victims of revenge pornography, those who choose to cast opinions upon them and some stakeholders tasked with their protection that, culturally, we are still not in a place where victims are taken seriously and the impact of non-consensually sharing is understood. Many victims will make excuses for the abuse they have received – they should not have taken the image in the first place, they consented to sharing once; therefore, they only have themselves to blame, the offender was exacting some sort of "revenge" in response to behaviour by the victim. Moreover, when observing commentary such as social media, offenders often feel like they have done nothing wrong, and they have that belief reinforced by peers. Even the term "revenge pornography" implies fault on the part of the victim and similar can be said about the wider problematic terminology.

Fundamentally, these crimes, and the impact on victims, centres on consent. It is not the image that causes offence or harm, it is the sharing of it in a manner that is uncontrolled and has no care for the welfare of the victim. While motivations for sharing might be diverse, and in some instances, offenders may argue that there is no intention to cause harm, their actions, and the non-consensual sharing, will, in a great many cases, cause harm. Therefore, any legislation should focus on harm to the victim, rather than the motive of the offender.

Chapters 4 and 5 have a detailed exploration of the current legislation, with a focus on the UK, around revenge pornography and teen sexting. They look both at the legislation in statute as well as how case law and sentencing is becoming established, while considering what aspects of the legislation work well and which parts are more problematic. Following this exploration, the final part of the book will explore in more detail where legislation requires development and how other stakeholders have a role to play in supporting victims and punishing offenders.

4   Where Is the Legislation?

This chapter will review attempts to define protection and prohibitive measures via legislation. While the chapter focuses upon recent developments in UK legislation, it will initially review previous legislation to highlight how the law has struggled to cope with socially disruptive technological facilitated phenomena. For example, the issues arising from the Protection of Children Act 1978 (the primary legislation for the prosecution of offences related to the manufacture and distribution of indecent images of a minor, which will be discussed in the second part of this chapter) have resulted in the prosecution of minors who have been the victims of the redistribution of self-generated images where the letter of the law has been applied. However, the law was developed at a time when the subject of the image could also be the taker of the image could not have been envisioned.

More recently, s33 of the UK's Criminal Justice and Courts Act 2015 created a new statutory offence of "disclosing private sexual photographs and films with intent to cause distress" (sometimes referred to as the "revenge pornography law") and the Serious Crime Bill 2015, which created a new offence of "sexual communication with a child", attempted to place the management of explicit self-generated images and criminal activity in a modern context. The chapter will also take a more philosophical position around what these pieces of legislation are actually trying to achieve – is this a prohibitive approach to chasing technology and disruptive social discourse or taking a more pragmatic perspective around the protection of potential victims? The chapter will also develop the exploration of law making to analyse how the legislation has been interpreted in the courts through case and sentencing analysis. While the focus of this chapter is on more recent legislation, consent will be explored in far more detail, particularly the interpretations in legal cases and the reporting of such. Anonymity will also be explored from the context of both victim and accused and the importance will be highlighted by drawing upon cases.

However, prior to this exploration, a consideration of some of the historical context and cases is made, which bring us to where we are today, as this helps to understand the routes to legislation.

A History of Revenge Porn Law

While the bespoke legislation around image-based abuse is (legally speaking) quite modern, the acts, along which the non-consensual sharing of images, have existed for far longer than the technology which made the self-generation of intimate images and their further distribution so straightforward and prevalent. While the first camera phones have only been available for around 20 years,[1] there were cases of "leaked" images being used to extort and control, and also gain financial benefit, long before digital images could be taken and shared so easily. The instant camera was first made commercially available in the 1940s and "Polaroid" cameras became very popular in the second half of the 20th century, although they were eventually usurped by the digital camera and then the camera phone. The instant camera could take "intimate" photographs without the potential embarrassment, or even legal action, that might result from the development of a camera film at a commercial photographic developing studio.

It should be no surprise, therefore, that instant camera images have been used to control. Perhaps the most famous early example was where images were used in the divorce case of the Duke and Duchess of Argyll in 1963.[2] In this case, the images in question were polaroid pictures of the duchess performing oral sex on an unidentified lover, and images of another man masturbating in the Duchess' rooms. While the images were used in the divorce case, they were considered so significant that they became part of a government investigation 40 years later in order to identify the males in the photographs.[3]

However, such images were not only the subject of society scandals. Through the 1980s, the American pornographic magazine Hustler ran a monthly feature called "beaver hunt", where readers would submit either images of themselves, or of a partner, along with some personal details such as hobbies, sexual interests and in some cases even their name. However, there were a number of lawsuits in the US, for example[4], that resulted from Hustler publishing images from people who claimed they had not consented to those images being shared and, in some instances, claimants stating that images had been stolen – in these cases, forged consent forms were said to have been used and claimants argued that the magazine had been negligent in checking consent and copyright of images prior to publication. And clearly, those who had submitted images fraudulently were doing so for financial gain – Hustler paid $50 for the publication of images.

The cases around Hustler are particularly interesting when looking at the development of legislation around the non-consensual sharing of images, given that challenges were made over the copyright of image and civil issues related to privacy. The non-consensual sharing of images is fundamental in the development

1 Wikipedia (n.d.). "Camera Phones". https://en.wikipedia.org/wiki/Camera_phone
2 Randell, D. (2013). "The scarlet Duchess of Argyll: Much more than just a Highland fling". *Independent.*   https://www.independent.co.uk/news/uk/home-news/the-scarlet-duchess-of-argyll-much-more-than-just-a-highland-fling-8498071.html
3 Hall, S. (2000). "'Headless men' in sex scandal finally named". *The Guardian.* https://www.theguardian.com/uk/2000/aug/10/sarahhall
4 5th Circuit (1984). "Wood V Hustler". https://www.leagle.com/decision/19841820736f2d108411634.xml

of "revenge porn" legislation but does not solely relate to intimate images in the past. Yet the issue around rights and ownership is fundamental.

Breach of Confidence

While the parliamentary debate and subsequent legislative developments focused on criminal law, civil claims have also been used to prevent the distribution of images.

The publication of private information without the consent of the subject gives rise to a potential cause of civil action in the form of a privacy or breach of confidence suit where the subject has a reasonable expectation of privacy. This would include the publication to third parties of private messages or photographs never intended to be shared with third parties, text messages and "sexts" or so-called revenge porn being common examples. Save where there is a public interest in the publication of some description of the private information, for example, by exposing the hypocrisy of a married public role model engaging in an affair, or where the subject themselves published the information, there will be limited defences and there will rarely be any justification for publication.

Privacy law has consistently been applied in relation to the sharing of images without consent. Peck vs UK 2003[5] centred on the infringement of the human rights of the applicant. In this case, the applicant was filmed on CCTV cameras owned by Brentwood Borough Council attempting to take his own life. While the attempt was unsuccessful, the council retrained the footage and subsequently released stills of the act (with no effort to hide the identity of the individual in the images) in promotional materials to demonstrate the effectiveness of CCTV and its use in public spaces. The applicant claimed that his right to privacy under Article 8 of the ECHR had been breached and also that his Article 13 rights (right to an effective remedy) had been affected due to the non-consensual nature of the sharing. The European Court of Human Rights found that a breach of Article 8 had been made.

When considering images and other media related to the non-consensual sharing of intimate material, two particular cases that stand out during this period between the widespread adoption of digital and camera phones, and legislation catching up with the use of such technology to abuse, are Contostavlos v Mendahun[6] and AMP v Persons unknown.[7]

In Contostavlos v Mendahun, the singer Tulisa Contostavlos obtained an interim injunction against the dissemination of a leaked sex tape which had been made available online. Continuing an interim injunction, Mr Justice Tugendhat commented that:

> details of a person's sexual life have thus been recognised for very many years as high on the list of matters which may be protected … It has also long

---

5 [2003] 36 EHRR 41.
6 [2012] EWHC 850.
7 [2011] EWHC 3454 (TCC).

been recognised that photographs are more intrusive than a verbal or written description. In the case of intrusive and intimate photographs of the kind in question in this case there is no real prospect of a defence of public domain.

In this case, the issue was arguably more significant because a video of the act had been shared, rather than simply photographs. While the case subsequently settled, in April 2012, an interim injunction was granted (continued in May) preventing the disclosure of photographs of a personal nature together with text messages sent by the claimant during the course of an adulterous affair with the second defendant. The photographs and text messages, described by the judge as "of a sexual nature, but could not be described as pornographic", had come into the control of the first defendant (with whom the second defendant had been in a relationship) in undisclosed circumstances. The court granted an order to protect the claimant's right to confidentiality and privacy, as well as to protect her from harassment.

AMP v Persons unknown was particularly significant because the injunction in this case was against "persons unknown" and attempted to control the spread of intimate images of the victim via digital, peer-to-peer file sharing and online channels where the sharer might only be recognised by their IP address. In this case, the applicant lost their mobile phone, which contained intimate images of her, and the series of images were subsequently shared online via peer-to-peer channels. The applicant was contacted on Facebook by someone who had obtained the images and threatened further dissemination if she did not add them as a friend on the social media platform. While the applicant ignored and deleted the messages, the abuser then contacted her father's business, again threatening to publish images. The images were subsequently shared via BitTorrent with the files prefixed with the applicant's name, so they were easily searchable. Applying the Harassment Act 1997, the judge felt there was sufficient evidence that the "unknown persons" had caused sufficient alarm and distress to the applicant and therefore an offence had been committed. As a result of the ruling, "persons unknown" could be tracked down by digital forensic specialists and instructed to remove the files. While jurisdictional issues would have presented some problems with this, it does at least afford some protection to the victim, who would have been able to use the court order to seek the removal of the files from web platforms.

It is fair to assume that a private citizen's reasonable expectation of privacy is appropriate in these cases, even though public opinion, as expressed in discussions of public debate in the previous chapter, might suggest that someone who discloses intimate images of themselves, or consents to having such images taken, is not in some way entitled to this expectation because, to quote opinions we frequently hear "if the victim hadn't have taken the pictures, the abuser would not have been able to share them". There has been some tension in some legislation in the US, for example, with state law in Texas,[8] that legislation preventing

---

8 Texas Judicial Branch (2018). "NO. 12-17-00346-CR" http://search.txcourts.go v/SearchMedia.aspx?MediaVersionID=204e054a-d329-4780-81ed-0603fd4d4fff &coa=coa12&DT=Opinion&MediaID=e2e7d674-d2ef-4ae7-a896-c8c3698be11b

the non-consensual sharing of intimate images is unconstitutional (arguing it restricted free speech). In the UK, while the reasonable expectation test was first defined in a case between a celebrity and media group,[9] there has been little legal exception, at the current time, to the view that Article 8 of the European Convention on Human Rights[10] is entirely appropriate in the context of image-based abuse and the consensual sharing of an image with a "trusted" individual does not telegraph consent to the recipient for them to share to whomever they wish.

Legislation Trying to Keep Up

Prior to the creation of the Criminal Justice and Courts Act 2015, the victims of the non-consensual sharing of intimate images had been forced to rely on various existing legislation never designed for the purpose. Typically:

- S1 of the Malicious Communications Act 1988.[11] Sending a communication that is grossly offensive, indecent, obscene, conveys a threat or is false, with intent to cause distress or anxiety
- S127 of the Communications Act 2003.[12] Sending a communication that is grossly offensive, indecent, obscene, menacing or false
- S2 and 4 of the Protection from Harassment Act 1997[13]

Or (as discussed above) the civil tort of misuse of private information or breach of confidence. However, other legislation has also been applied in different circumstances:

- Section 21, Theft Act 1968[14] (blackmail). Where stolen images have been used to blackmail
- Section 154 Criminal Justice and Public Order Act 1994.[15] Causing intentional harassment, alarm or distress

---

9 [2004] 2 AC 457 [21].
10 ECHR (2019). "European Convention on Human Rights Article 8". https://www.echr.coe .int/Documents/Guide_Art_8_ENG.pdf
11 UK Government (1988). "Section 1, Malicious Communications Act 1988)". http://www .legislation.gov.uk/ukpga/1988/27/section/1/2004-10-31
12 UK Government (2003). "Section 127, Communications Act 2003". http://www.legislati on.gov.uk/ukpga/2003/21/section/127/enacted
13 UK Government (1997). "Protection from Harassment Act 1997". http://www.legislati on.gov.uk/ukpga/1997/40/contents
14 UK Government (1968). "Section 21, Theft Act 1968". http://www.legislation.gov.uk/ ukpga/1968/60/section/21
15 UK Government (1994). "Section 154 Criminal Justice & Public Order Act 1994". http:// www.legislation.gov.uk/ukpga/1994/33/section/154

- Section 1 of the Computer Misuse Act 1990.[16] Where the images have been obtained through unauthorised access to computer equipment

Furthermore, when the victim is a minor, the below legislation related to child protection has been used, and this will be discussed in more detail later in this chapter:

- Section 1, Protection of Children Act 1978[17]
- Section 15a, Sexual Offences Act 2003[18]

As can be seen, the legislation, while being used to address the impacts of the non-consensual sharing of intimate images, was often being applied in a manner for which it was either not intended or not entirely, or indeed at all, fit for purpose (something to which we will return when considering minor on minor sexting).

Drawing from the literature discussed in Chapter 3, the profiling of victims can focus on women as the abused and males as offenders. Indeed, a lot of the early debate around the need for legislation in the UK Parliament centred upon the need for new laws to protect women from these crimes. With a brief exploration of the transcripts of the debate, there are a number of instances that highlight the stereotype of male offender/female victim. In an early stage in the debate, Maria Miller MP, a politician instrumental in what become section 33 of the Criminal Justice and Courts Act 2015, made that very point.[19]

Maria Miller (Basingstoke) (Con)

I asked for this debate because of the growing problem faced by adult women in this country who have had sexually explicit pictures of themselves posted online without their knowledge and without their consent on dedicated websites, readily promoted by search engines such as Google and Yahoo. These are ordinary women who have been in loving relationships in which nude or sexually explicit pictures have been taken in private, something that is not illegal. When that relationship goes wrong, their partner's revenge is to post on the internet intimate pictures taken over the course of that relationship as well as distributing them to employers, families and friends.

---

16 UK Government (1990). "Section 1 Computer Misuse Act 1990". http://www.legislati on.gov.uk/ukpga/1990/18/section/1
17 Ibid.
18 Ibid.
19 UK Parliament (2014). "Hansard – House of Commons Debates June 19 June 2014 – Revenge Porn". https://publications.parliament.uk/pa/cm201415/cmhansrd/cm14 0619/debtext/140619-0004.htm#14061947000003

The experience was first raised with me by a constituent. In my constituent's words this bullying behaviour or harassment – perhaps we should call it sexual abuse –

"leaves the victim feeling powerless – it can result in that person losing their career, damaging their future job prospects and devastating their relationships". […]

The term "revenge pornography" has been used to describe these actions, but however we refer to them, they have to be recognised as the abhorrent crimes they are, which take place mostly but not exclusively against women.

It is interesting to note that early in the debate it was raised that victims of non-consensual sharing can lose their careers and their future job prospects can be damaged, as this is something that discussions with the Revenge Porn Helpline have also raised. Indeed, those at the helpline helped inform this debate. However, while raised in the debate, this issue was never developed further or considered in the final legislation – the legislation seems to rely more on abuser motivation than impact upon the victim.

It was also interesting to note that there was much debate around whether new legislation was actually needed, and existing pieces of legislation were raised in terms of the law that might already protect victims, including:

* Obscene Publications Act 1959[20]
* Protection of Children Act 1978[21]
* Malicious Communications Act 1988[22]
* Computer Misuse Act 1990[23]
* Protection from Harassment Act 1997[24]
* Communications Act 2003[25]

In reflecting on the discussion in the debate, it seemed clear that, as with a great deal of online abuse-related crime, fitting "pre-Internet" legislation to the problem space was, in itself, problematic. The Protection of Children Act 1978, a particularly problematic piece of legislation when it comes to image-based abuse among minors, has been applied to addressing the non-consensual sharing of images when the victim is below the age of majority, equally, if applied correctly, the producer of the image (i.e. the victim) is also subject to prosecution.

20 UK Government (1959). "Obscene Publications Act 1959". http://www.legislation.go v.uk/ukpga/Eliz2/7-8/66/contents
21 Ibid.
22 Ibid.
23 Ibid.
24 Ibid.
25 Ibid.

The application of obscenity regulation is also a curious one – the thresholds for what constitutes obscenity are high (does it "deprave and corrupt" persons who see, read or hear it) and while the interpretation of obscenity is left to the discretion of the courts, a lot of "revenge pornography" would fall far short of this categorisation. Furthermore, only content that is grossly offensive, indecent, obscene or menacing would fall under the Communications Act (section 127).

The use of "technological" legislation such as the Computer Misuse Act is interesting but also severely limited (the legislation is deeply flawed and in dire need of an update itself) – the reference to the act was in relation to section 1, which makes it an offence to access data held on a device without authorisation. Again, there might be a time when an image or video is stolen from a victim's device (or online storage) but this would be in the minority. Sadly, it is more frequent for the victim to have consented to share the media with the person who subsequently goes on to distribute it further.

Finally, harassment, which requires a course of conduct, also has its limits with this sort of offence because these might be one-off acts, rather than a persistent campaign of abuse.

Nevertheless, the debate does raise an important issue in terms of the balance between the establishment of new legislation and repurposing of existing statute when we are to consider the protection of victims from "online" offences.

There is a risk to suggest that when a new type of offence arises that is technologically facilitated that there is a need for new legislation alongside it. One can see from this debate that there were a number of pieces of legislation that *could* have been relevant, although all fall short of the protection needed by victims. However, the gap in the legislation is less to do with the technology itself and more that there is nothing on the statute books that adequately provides provision for the protection of victims where personal images of an intimate nature are shared non-consensually. This is an important point to note – the technology is not the issue, non-consensual sharing is.

Subsequent debate at the amendment state of the draft bill also brought up the need for the protection of women in this new legislation:[26]

Maria Miller MP

I have been campaigning on behalf of women who have contacted me to get a change in the law to make posting revenge pornography a crime, and today we have a chance to make a change that will literally transform the future for many people in our country.

26 UK Parliament (2014). "Hansard – House of Commons Debates 01 December 2014 – Criminal Justice and Courts Bill". https://hansard.parliament.uk/Commons/2014-12 -01/debates/14120129000001/CriminalJusticeAndCourtsBill

Mrs Miller also repeated an often-heard mantra from governments, particularly in more recent times:[27]

> The law must keep up to date with the ever-evolving changes and challenges thrown down to us by the internet and digital technology. **What is illegal offline is illegal online**, but the impact of having a nude or sexually explicit image posted on the internet for thousands or even millions of people to see is entirely different from the impact of a similar image being distributed offline, and I believe that the law should reflect that.

As highlighted above, sometimes this online/offline distinction is an artificial one that results in calls to address this "technological" crime with a technological solution. Within the debates, there were indeed calls for service providers to implement technical solutions to address this. While a later chapter in this text explores the role of the service provider in more detail, it is worthwhile to note here:

> Maria Miller MP
>
> If websites are hosted in more obscure countries, splash pages should be used to block illegal pornography images from being viewed in the UK in exactly the same way as they have been used to block child abuse images.

The intention of this technological innovation is an earnest one – if websites hosting revenge pornography images are hosted in countries beyond the reach of UK law, the service providers within the UK should, in the same way as currently happens with sites hosting child abuse images, provide a splash page to warn the viewer of the sort of content they are about to access. However, as pointed out by another parliamentarian in the debate, this is not always a clear cut as it seems:

> Dr Julian Huppert MP (Cambridge) (Lib Dem)
>
> Although the right hon. Lady spoke about automatic processes to filter these things out, there will be challenges. The work of the Internet Watch Foundation – I declare an interest as one of its champions – on child abuse images is fantastic, but it cannot be directly mapped on to images of revenge porn, because the images themselves are not the issue; it is about intent and consent.

If one is to consider technological interventions against child abuse images, it is very clear that this content is illegal and should be either taken down or blocked

---

27 UK Government (2019). "Online Harms White Paper". https://assets.publishing.service. gov.uk/government/uploads/system/uploads/attachment_data/file/793360/Online_ Harms_White_Paper.pdf

from access, something, as Mr Huppert mentions, is done effectively by the Internet Watch Foundation in the UK, whose key operational objective is the removal of illegal child abuse images from the internet.[28] However, in the case of revenge pornography, this is less clear. As discussed above, the thresholds for the illegality of adult content are far beyond what is often shared as revenge pornography. It is the act of *non-consensual sharing* that causes the content to become illegal, and this is extremely difficult for an algorithm to determine without some level of metadata (that currently does not exist) in the image or video file itself to show that consent has been granted. An algorithm has no way (indeed, neither does a human) to determine, through inspection of the image, whether this is one that has been shared without consent. While there are technological interventions that are technically capable and operationally realistic for service providers to implement (and are discussed in Chapter 6), blanket prevention from access to content that is not, of itself, illegal is not one of them. In the same debate Dr Huppert continued by making a very important point we will return to in a subsequent chapter:

Dr Huppert

For me, this is fundamentally an issue not about revenge or pornography – the term "revenge porn" is not ideal – but about consent. We need a system where, particularly through education, we get people to understand what consent is about: what can be agreed to and what cannot be agreed. Whether it is sexual assault and physical violence, emotional assault or the taking and spreading of such images, it should be about whether consent has been given. That is the education I would like to see.

This is not an issue technology can solve. And while it might be impossible to remove completely, it can be tackled with effective legislation and effective education around consent, something discussed in more detail in Chapter 7.

Criminal Law

Returning to criminal law, the outcome of the debates was that there was a need to develop legislation specific to image-based abuse and the non-consensual sharing of images. Section 33 of the Criminal Justice and Courts Bill was developed.

Section 33 of the Criminal Justice and Courts Act 2015 came into force on 13 April 2015, creating a new criminal offence of disclosing private sexual photographs and films with intent to cause distress. Crucial to the offence are: (a) the lack of consent of the individual appearing in the photograph and film; and (b) the intent to cause that individual distress. The offence carries a maximum two-year sentence on conviction.

---

28 https://www.iwf.org.uk/

The fundamental wording of the act states:

33 Disclosing private sexual photographs and films with intent to cause distress
 (1) It is an offence for a person to disclose a private sexual photograph or film if the disclosure is made—
  (a) without the consent of an individual who appears in the photograph or film, and
  (b) with the intention of causing that individual distress.

Intent is a fundamental issue with this legislation. Subsection 8 clarifies this is:

A person charged with an offence under this section is not to be taken to have disclosed a photograph or film with the intention of causing distress merely because that was a natural and probable consequence of the disclosure.

One cannot presume intent, one must prove it. As with all offences requiring proof of intent, the foresight of the probability of a consequence does not of itself amount to intention but may be evidence of it (see[29,30,31] and the Supreme Court's decision in[32]).

This is further underlined with guidance from the Crown Prosecution Service:[33]

A person will only be guilty of the offence if the reason for disclosing the photograph, or one of reasons, is to cause distress to a person depicted in the photograph or film.

And the College of Policing:[34]

For the offence to be committed, the disclosure must take place without the consent of at least one of those featured in the disclosed picture and with the intention of causing that person distress

Intention to cause distress must be proved, and therefore, provides an immediate, potential defence. Further aspects of defence include:

1. Disclosing to the subject of the image only
2. Disclosure is necessary for crime prevention

29 Moloney [1985] AC 905.
30 Woolin [1999] AC 82.
31 Hancock [1986] AC 455.
32 Jogee [2016] 2 WLR 681.
33 Crown Prosecution Service (2017). "Revenge Pornography – Guidelines on prosecuting the offence of Disclosing Private Sexual Photographs and films". https://www.cps.gov.uk/legal-g uidance/revenge-pornography-guidelines-prosecuting-offence-disclosing-private-sexual
34 College of Policing (2015). "Revenge Pornography Briefing Note – May 2015".http://lib rary.college.police.uk/docs/appref/briefing-note-revenge-pornography-may-2015.pdf

3. Public interest
4. The defendant believed the material was already in the public domain

Intent

As set out above, a crucial element of the offence is the intent to cause distress to the subject of the photographs or film. So, a user simply retweeting or forwarding an image would only fall under s33 if the intent was to cause distress.

In many cases, the intent is fairly evident, with many offenders admitting that they posted the images in retaliation for a perceived wrongdoing by the victim. To date, surprisingly few cases are emerging where the alleged offender has relied on the absence of intent in their defence. In July 2016, Christopher Green of Banbury, Oxfordshire, pleaded guilty to the offence, after forwarding a video showing his former partner performing a sexual act.[35] He had received the video from another of her former boyfriends, Aidan Farrelly of Hatfield, Hertfordshire, who later admitted to having sent the video out of revenge. By contrast, Green had forwarded it to his former partner and her best friend to warn her that it was being circulated. He also reported the video to the police. Green received a conditional discharge and an order to pay £250 costs; Farrelly, a two-month sentence (suspended for 12 months), 100 hours unpaid work and also £250 in costs.

While Green's decision to send not only a warning but the video itself to the best friend may have been foolish or misconceived at best (that being the only offence committed; it was not an offence to disclose back to the subject (s33(2)), his account of his intention was seemingly accepted by the prosecution. That is reflected in the very low sentence imposed. But it is unclear why Green should have pleaded guilty at all if his intention was to warn, rather than to cause distress. The act is clear, and s33(8) emphasises the distinction between the offender's intention and the consequences of his actions. Although these sorts of circumstance are likely to be few and far between, the requirement to prove intention is an important threshold and it is unlikely that Parliament intended to criminalise those who act as Mr Green did.

Anonymity

The "intent" behind the crime has also been used in the argument over whether the victims of the offence should receive anonymity, a protection automatically

---

35 Mail Online (2016). "Advertising salesman, 34, is hauled before the courts for 'sending revenge porn' after tipping off his ex that another of her boyfriends had sent him a sex tape of her". *The Daily Mail.* https://www.dailymail.co.uk/news/article-3706525/Advertising -salesmen-34-hauled-courts-sending-revenge-porn-tipping-ex-boyfriends-sent-sex-tape-h er.html

accorded to the victims of "sexual crimes". In a letter to North Yorkshire Crime Commissioner Julia Mulligan, then Policing Minister Mike Penning[36] stated:

[The new offence] is not a sexual offence, that is to say that the mental element of the offence is not a sexual one, it is a malicious one (the intent to cause distress). The behaviour itself is also not "sexual", although the material disclosed may be sexual in nature, the offences committed requires, for example, no element of sexual contact, sexual intent or sexual gratification.

Instead it is the disclosure of photographs and/or films without the consent of the person appearing in them. In this way, the offence is more akin to the existing malicious communications offence or to blackmail than it is to a sexual offence.

The government's position has remained consistent, Karen Bradley, then Minister for Preventing Abuse, Exploitation and Crime, writing in June 2016:[37]

Whilst victims can in some circumstances feel violated by the malicious disclosure of sexual images the offence is not a sexual one.

It does not require any element of sexual contact or sexual gratification and it does not attract sex offender registration ... We do not consider automatic anonymity is necessary or desirable in the case of revenge pornography.

While orders have been made in individual cases, campaigners argue that the prospect of being named in the courts is dissuading many victims from coming forward. In June 2019, it was announced that the Law Commission would review anonymity for revenge porn victims, with their report due in the summer of 2021.[38] This is certainly an area in which there is likely to be continued campaigning.

However, from a victim-centric perspective, as experienced by those who work at the Revenge Porn Helpline, they are very clear that anonymity is appropriate (given the impact on the victims and the fact that there is clearly a sexual element to these crimes – the impact is exacerbated as a result of the images being disseminated are intimate, and this is the motivation for harm), and needed if we

---

36 Police Professional (2016). "PCC Hits Back At Disturbing Government Response to Revenge Porn Campaign". https://www.policeprofessional.com/news/pcc-hits-back-a t-%C2%91disturbing%C2%92-government-response-to-revenge-porn-campaign/
37 Laville, S. (2016). "'Revenge porn' victims Should Get Anonymity, say 75% of people". *The Guardian*. https://www.theguardian.com/law/2016/jul/19/revenge-porn-victims-shoul d-get-anonymity-say-75-per-cent-of-people
38 UK Government (2019). "Law around Non-Consensual Taking, making and sharing of Sexual Images to be reviewed". https://www.gov.uk/government/news/law-around-non-consensual-taking-making-and-sharing-of-sexual-images-to-be-reviewed

are to get more victims making complaints and receiving effective support during the criminal justice process. Recent reporting on the review into the legislation made this clear.[39]

Third-Party Liability

According to the information revealed to the BBC under their FOI requests in the above report, the site most frequently used by perpetrators to distribute images is Facebook, appearing in 68% of cases. Instagram appeared in 12% of cases and Snapchat 5%. Twitter appeared in 14 cases, with mobile phones only being cited in eight cases and WhatsApp in 16. At least two cases involved print copies being distributed, one defendant distributing intimate pictures at a super-market and another in public places around a North Somerset town.

Although the act imposed no liability on third parties hosting the images, websites were swift to see the reputational benefit in being seen to be proac-tive in helping the victims, many setting up specific forms for users to report revenge porn. In just one example, Microsoft reported that in 2019,[40] there were 611 removal requests for "non-consensual pornography" from its Bing search engine, OneDrive online storage system and Xbox Live, of which it accepted 566, a 92.6% acceptance rate. Based on Microsoft's half-yearly reporting, Table 4.1

Table 4.1 Non-Consensual Pornography Removal Requests on Microsoft Platforms since July 2015

	Requests reported	Requests accepted	Percentage of requests accepted
July–Dec 2019	344	317	92.15%
Jan–June 2019	267	249	93.26%
July–Dec 2018	212	124	58.00%
Jan–June 2018	362	242	66.85%
July–Dec 2017	438	271	61.87%
Jan–June 2017	608	344	56.58%
Jul–Dec 2016	580	298	51.38%
Jan–Jun 2016	407	251	61.67%
July–Dec 2015	537	338	62.94%

Source: Microsoft Content Removal Reports.

39 BBC News (2019). "Revenge Porn Laws 'Not Working', Says Victims Group". *BBC News*. https://www.bbc.co.uk/news/uk-4830975
40 Microsoft (2019). "Content Removal Requests Report". https://www.microsoft.com/en-us/corporate-responsibility/content-removal-requests-report

shows the number of reports and takedowns for "non-consensual pornography removal requests" since the introduction of the legislation.[41]

Nevertheless, the onus on third-party liability continues to grow, even if the government struggles to shape it. In April 2019, the UK government released its "Online Harms" White Paper[42] proclaiming it will ensure that the UK is "the safest place in the world to go online". It aimed to set out both the problem domains and solutions, which included a regulatory framework, an independent regulator for "online safety", the scope of companies within this framework, how enforcement might work, the role of technology and the empowerment of the end-user.

The Origins of Teen Sexting and the Law

As has already been considered in previous chapters, the legislation applied to minors exchanging (consensually and non-consensually) images was established many years ago. The use of legislation around teen sexting focuses on the act of manufacturing and distribution of an indecent image of a minor, with nothing in the legislation to consider the "self-generated" nature of the content.

The foundation of the legislation, the Protection of Children Act 1978, makes it illegal for someone to generate and distribute an indecent image of a child. Clearly, in the event of self-generation and sharing, the victim will also be perpetrator under this legislation. The legislation was introduced and debated before a time when someone might self-generate an intimate image of themselves from their bedroom and have it passed around many recipients with the touch of a button could have ever been envisioned.

From a punitive perspective, within the legislation, teen sexting is unambiguously illegal under s1 PCA:

it is an offence for a person—

(a) to take, or permit to be taken [or to make], any indecent photograph [or pseudo-photograph] of a child…; or

(b) to distribute or show such indecent photographs [or pseudo-photographs]; or

(c) to have in his possession such indecent photographs [or pseudo-photographs], with a view to their being distributed or shown by himself or others; or

(d) to publish or cause to be published any advertisement likely to be understood as conveying that the advertiser distributes or shows such indecent photographs [F4 or pseudo-photographs], or intends to do so.

---

41 Microsoft are reporting on worldwide requests, but the data is a good illustration on the confidence of victims to submit requests, and the change in acceptance of these requests over time.

42 Ibid.

This legislation would clearly demand charge when applied to a minor self-producing an intimate image. If we consider Foucault's views of the role of the police,[43] he recognises their role as part of the punitive, rather than restorative, process – they collect evidence, they enforce the law and they facilitate the punishment considered appropriate by society. It is not down to the enforcers of the law to make subjective judgements and whether the law is an ass.

However, given the year that the law reached ascent, it could not have been in the minds of the legislators that the subject of the image, the taker of the image and the distributor of the image could all be the same person. The motivation for the legislation arose from an "obscenity" campaigner, Mary Whitehouse,[44] whose lobbying resulted in a Private Member's Bill by the Bexleyheath Member of Parliament Cyril Townsend, whose obituary by former MP Tam Dalyell,[45] specifically states that:

> He was prescient in his worries about child pornography and the sexual exploitation of children and in 1978 secured the passage into law of a private member's bill on the Protection of Children.

Indeed, if one explores Hansard to review the debate around the development of the bill, it is clear that the focus was on the protection of children from exploitation by adult pornographers. In his introduction of the bill before Parliament, Mr Townsend very clearly specified this legislation was to tackle the production of "child pornography":

> Mr Cyril D. Townsend (Bexleyheath) (Con)[46]
>
> Child pornography is a distasteful subject to debate. Not unnaturally, the vast majority of our fellow countrymen are not fully aware of its prevalence in these islands, for much of the trade is kept under the counter. But right hon. and hon. Members appreciate from their postbags that there is much growing public anxiety and strong pressure for legislation action. Half a million people have already signed a petition calling for a change in the law. We have a duty to look into the sewers of our society. We have a duty to provide penalties for those who abuse our tolerance and our freedoms. Above all, we have a duty to protect innocent children.

43 Foucault, M. (1975). *Discipline and punish.* A. Sheridan, Tr. Paris, FR: Gallimard.
44 Thompson, B. (2012). *Ban this Filth – Letters from the Mary Whitehouse Archive.* Faber and Faber.
45 Tam Dalyell (2013). "Obituary - Sir Cyril Townsend: Member of Parliament". *Independent.* https://www.independent.co.uk/news/obituaries/sir-cyril-townsend-member-of-parliament-8974043.html
46 Hansard (1978). "10 February 1978. Volume 943. Column 1827". http://bit.ly/381qjNF

Within the debate the focus is entirely on protecting children from abuse and exploitation in the production of pornography:

Rev. Ian Paisley (Antrim, North)[47] (DUP)

The House should keep before it the fact that we are dealing with the welfare of the child. This is not a debate on pornography per se; it is a debate on the taking of a child and the ruining of it for financial purposes so that the child's future is so twisted and warped that it is destroyed in time and eternity.

Mr George Rogers (Chorley)[48] (Lab)

The purpose of the Bill is to stop up the loopholes in the laws which are designed to protect children from abuse. It is apparent that the measure has generated wide support inside and outside the Chamber. The opening words of the Bill carry, for me at least, a deep appeal. They read:

"A Bill to prevent the exploitation of children".
I find that immensely heart-warming.

Mr. Robert Hicks (Bodmin)[49] (Con)

On this occasion I wish my hon. Friend the Member for Bexleyheath every good fortune in his second attempt to get a Private Member's Bill on the statute book. His choice of subject reflects a widespread public concern. In the seven years that I have been a Member of this House I can recall only one previous occasion on which I have had as many letters and petitions on a social issue. The previous occasion had to do with the Abortion (Amendment) Bill in 1971.

I appreciate that there are widely differing attitudes towards pornography generally. On the other hand, no one in the House dissents from the proposition that children should not be involved at any stage, since they are specially vulnerable and are not able fully to realise what they are doing or consent to what they do when involved in this despicable activity. At times I find difficulty in defining my attitude towards those areas and instances where legislation should be introduced to protect people against themselves and their own actions. This is very much a grey area, as has been suggested. In terms of the exploitation of children I find myself in no such difficulty.

There was similar focus when the bill reached debate in the House of Lords.

---

47 Hansard (1978). "10 February 1978. Volume 943. Column 1867". http://bit.ly/30en56U
48 Hansard (1978). "10 February 1978. Volume 943. Column 1885". http://bit.ly/2sjEdvl
49 Hansard (1978). "10 February 1978. Volume 943. Column 1889". http://bit.ly/3afBUL8

The Earl of Longford[50] (Lab)

I should like to express great concern about the proposed new Clause 1(4) (a). I am not dealing with a narrow legal point but with quite a broad point. Some of your Lordships may have read what Mrs. Whitehouse wrote in The Times this morning. After all, she has some standing in this matter because she and our organisation were the initiators of a campaign against child pornography.

Lord Robertson of Oakridge[51]

I welcome this Bill because it recognises that boys and girls under 16 need protection from those who would exploit their vulnerability and abuse their trust. May T [sic.] join in thanking those who identified the gap in the law protecting children in this respect, those who alerted and mobilised public opinion and those who reacted to this by assisting the passage of the Bill so far. May I take this chance to pay tribute to the noble Baroness, Lady Faithfull, for the way in which she introduced the Bill.

Viscount Barrington[52]

The purpose of the Bill is to protect children, and I think that is the point we want to remember. As I said, children have always been here and have always needed protection. Without taking up too much of your Lordships' time, I would take you back to ancient Carthage, where children needed protection from being put into a furnace for the honour of Moloch, the god of power, or even as far back as the Shaftesbury Acts of the last century, when it took a very long time, with some opposition in your Lordships' House, to prevent children from working in factories – often with the consent of their parents – for I forget how many hours a day in circumstances that we need not go into now. That was sacrificing children to Mammon.

   I think most of us would agree that both of those were wrong, but now— and I do not think there is any need to produce evidence here, though it can be produced —children are being sacrificed to the god of pornogra- phy and/or sex. I do not know who that is. Perhaps it is Eros. I doubt if it is Aphrodite. But there I do not doubt that the menace facing us at the moment is the flood of "liberalism", which is one word used, though speak- ing as a Liberal I dislike that use of the word.

The nature of all of the debate around the bill was that children required legis- lation to ensure they were not exploited by adults wishing to exploit them for sexual and financial gain. This was the sole motivation for the introduction of this

50 Hansard (1978). "18 May 1978 Volume 392 Column 547". http://bit.ly/2sZVvhm
51 Hansard (1978). "18 May 1978 Volume 392 Column 565". http://bit.ly/2R98BB4
52 Hansard (1978). "18 May 1978 Volume 392 Column 572". http://bit.ly/2uKJbCk

legislation, and it was effective up to the point that a minor could have sufficient technology at their disposal to self-produce images.

However, in the modern digital world, we have a legislative tension between, on the one hand, protecting the victim and, on the other, addressing the illegality of the generation and sharing. However, is a minor who chooses to self-produce an image and send it to another minor a victim of exploitation or one being abused in the production of pornography? Clearly, there are some scenarios when there might be coercion or threat in the minor making the image or video of themselves, but the law still calls for the producer of the image (the minor) to be prosecuted due to the wording of the legislation.

This chapter has explored the legislation and its evolution related to both the non-consensual sharing of intimate images among adults and minors. There is a clear distinction between, for adults, a piece of legislation developed in a time when there was at least awareness of the facilitation of these acts on digital platforms, and for minors, the application of legislation being used in scenarios in which it was never intended. Regardless of the efficacy of the legislation for adults, it does, at least, focus on the protection of the victim and the prosecution of the abuser. With the legislation for minors, the victim has no such protection and is, by the letter of the law, as liable for prosecution as the abuser.

Chapter 5 explores the efficacy of this legislation by drawing from primary data sources and also considering the implications from secondary data.

5 Is the Legislation Working?

The previous chapter has explored the legislation in d epth and considered how it is being applied in case law. Clearly, the legislation is being applied and, in some cases, it is effective. Nevertheless, is it also clear that in certain cases, it is not performing its intended role,[1] and in some cases (particularly related to the exchange of indecent images among minors), it can be used to revictimise a vulnerable victim because they have, in the eyes of the law, committed an offence. As have already raised, there are challenges in the view that at the present time, with revenge pornography viewed as a communication rather than a sexual crime, the protections afforded to the victim in sexual crimes (such as anonymity) are causing some victims to withhold or withdraw complaints. Many clients of the Revenge Porn Helpline disclose they have only come to them as a last resort – it would be preferable that the criminal justice environment and public awareness was such that they would recognise the abuse to which they have been subjected and make a complaint immediately. However, with the harm that results from the knowledge that images have been shared, and are potentially viewable by many people online or that they are being sent to targeted individuals with a relationship to the victim, the lack of anonymity if the case was brought and enters into the public domain is clearly a deterrent for disclosure. Moreover, as discussed in previous chapters, the need to demonstrate either intention to harm or sexual gratification also present challenges for moving to prosecute.

In this chapter, through empirical evidence as well as legislative analysis, consideration is made concerning where the law is effective and where it is not sufficient. It will draw, once more, from discussions with the Revenge Pornography Helpline, as well as other empirical work with children and young people and also data from government sources. The case presented in this chapter is that, even if fully effective, legislation is not enough. If it lacks effectiveness, there are further concerns. After considering flaws in legislation, and the risk of those flaws being repeated again, we will return to the broader social concerns around self-generation and victim blaming, particularly around the recent upskirting debates,

---

1 BBC (2018). "Revenge porn: One in Three Allegations Dropped". *BBC News.* https://www.bbc.co.uk/news/uk-england-44411754

before casting a more focused analysis on the wider stakeholder perspectives in Chapter 6.

Building on the discussion in Chapter 3 around interviews with the Revenge Porn Helpline and analysis of the case book, further analysis explores specifically how the law helped and presented challenges to them. A good jumping-off point to this chapter is to consider the views presented and how this ties up with the effectiveness of the legislation. Once this response has been explored, and associated evidence bases to illustrate the issues raised, similar consideration with the legislation around teen sexting will be made, which, while overlapping, is more openly problematic.

What Does the Revenge Porn Helpline Need?

In considering the impact of legislation, the staff at the helpline were asked a general question – "What do you need from the legislation to help you and your clients?" This did result in an interesting discussion about the role of legislation in the safeguarding of victims and the punishment of offenders.

A central point in the discussion is that while the "revenge pornography" legislation was a step forward, having new legislation sometimes is not enough, particularly when it does not fully encapsulate the problem. In the view of the helpline staff (an opinion shared by many scholars[2]), the legislation should centre squarely around revenge pornography being a form of abuse. At the present time, the focus on the act of "Disclosing private sexual photographs and films with intent to cause distress" seems to focus more on the motivation of the abuser than the impact on the victim, which seems contradictory to the motivation of the legislation. The impact of the sharing of these images on the victim has already been discussed – it is distressing for them and it is something that can have a serious long-term impact on their lives and their mental wellbeing. Their feeling was that the legislation should reflect the often cruel nature of the action, and the fact that the sharing can be part of wider abusive, rather than isolating the legislation on the act of sharing.

The role of threat related to the non-consensual sharing of images has also been explored previously – a lot of this abuse relates to power over the victim. While they might, in some cases, have chosen to terminate a relationship, the ex-partner wishes to still have control over them, and the non-consensual sharing of intimate images is one way of achieving this. However, if the goal is one of power and control, what is more controlling? The sharing of an image or the threat to share an image? Once the image has been shared, at some level, the control exerted over the victim dissipates – the image has been shared, the impact has been felt. While it is acknowledged that with digital artefacts it is possible to share

---

2 McGlynn, C., and Rakley, E. (2016). "Not 'Revenge Porn', But Abuse: Let's Call It Image-Based Sexual Abuse". https://inherentlyhuman.wordpress.com/2016/02/15/not-revenge-porn-but-abuse-lets-call-it-image-based-sexual-abuse/

repeatedly, and threaten to share repeatedly, once an image has been shared, the abuser does potentially expose themselves to punishment, whereas, currently, the victim has less course for redress if the abuser is threatening to share.

By way of contrast, the equivalent legislation in Scottish law, the Abusive Behaviour and Sexual Harm (Scotland) Act 2016[3] makes specific mention of threat:

Disclosing, or threatening to disclose, an intimate photograph or film

(1) A person ("A") commits an offence if—

   (a) A discloses, **or threatens to disclose**, a photograph or film which shows, or appears to show, another person ("B") in an intimate situation,

   (b) by doing so, A intends to cause B fear, alarm or distress or A is reckless as to whether B will be caused fear, alarm or distress, and

   (c) the photograph or film has not previously been disclosed to the public at large, or any section of the public, by B or with B's consent.

This legislation was enacted in July 2017 and the Scottish Government's annual crime reporting showed[4] there were 421 crimes recorded against the legislation between September 2017 and September 2018 and 596 recorded the following year, clearly showing the legislation is being used. Note also that Scotland lists this as a sexual crime.

Returning to civil claims, while the victim does have a legal claim to the images if they produced them themselves, this route is far less likely to allow them to take back control from the abuser because such a claim to copyright would generally be a civil case, and therefore, not something that would attract the attention of the police. The issue of civil claims was raised with one member of staff, who said she had not spoken to a single person who had expressed any desire to pursue a civil claim against an abuser. While this might be due to the lack of knowledge around copyright and privacy breaches, it was observed that in most cases, the victim did not wish to win damages against their abuser, they wanted them to be punished and learn that their behaviour was unacceptable or, as this was stated by the member of staff "education tempered with a large dose of punishment". Many will simply wish to remove the images from public circulation. More recently, there has been one high profile civil case in the UK where YouTube celebrity Chrissy Chambers used breach of confidence to receive "substantial damages" against an ex-partner who shared videos of them having sex (which were reported to have been filmed without her consent) on various

3 Scottish Government (2016). "Abusive Behaviour and Sexual Harm (Scotland) Act 2016". https://www.legislation.gov.uk/asp/2016/22/section/2/enacted
4 Scottish Government (2018). "Recorded Crime in Scotland 2018-19". https://www.gov .scot/publications/recorded-crime-scotland-2018-19/

pornography sites.[5] This was reported as a "landmark case", where she sued for harassment, breach of confidence and misuse of private information, although it followed a similar approach to Contostavlos v Mendahun.[6]

The lack of legislation around edited or photoshopped images was also a concern for the helpline, given they deal with clients where abusers have carried out these practices. With the sophistication of image and video editing, it can sometimes to be difficult to identify a fake image, and therefore, the abuser can cause harm to the victim without ever needing legitimate intimate images of them. With the emergence of algorithm-based human image synthesis techniques (sometimes referred to as "deep fakes"[7]), increasingly realistic images, and even videos, can now be produced. As such, the helpline staff were clear that "pseudo-sexual" imagery should be part of the legislation and they had spoken to clients who had been subject to abuse from these sorts of images. By way of comparison, the production of pseudo-sexual images of children has been made illegal in amendments to the Protection of Children Act 1978 that took place as part of the Criminal Justice and Public Order Act in 1994.[8] While the wording of the legislation now seems somewhat old fashioned:

"Pseudo-photograph" means an image, whether made by computer-graphics or otherwise howsoever, which appears to be a photograph.

It does provide protection to minors that is not afforded to adult victims of these sort of acts.

Staff also felt that it is important for new legislation to be effective because the application of old laws in this context often falls short. For example, it was viewed that Malicious Communications were too old to deal with revenge pornography crimes effectively due to the ambiguity of what constitutes "indecency" in a communication or the high threshold for "grossly offensive" – many of the images shared in revenge pornography cases in order to abuse the victim might not be considered intimate (and certainly not grossly offensive); in the eyes of the law, however, the harm to the victim can still be significant. Harassment was also viewed as ineffective, mainly due to the need for repeated behaviours for an act to

5 Kellman, J. (2018). "YouTube Star Wins Damages in landmark UK 'Revenge Porn' Case". *The Guardian.* https://www.theguardian.com/technology/2018/jan/17/youtube-star-c hrissy-chambers-wins-damages-in-landmark-uk-revenge-porn-case
6 Ibid.
7 Chesney, R., and Citron, D. (2018). "Deep Fakes: A Looming Challenge for Privacy, Democracy, and National Security" (July 14, 2018). 107 California Law Review (2019, Forthcoming); U of Texas Law, Public Law Research Paper No. 692; U of Maryland Legal Studies Research Paper No. 2018-21. Available at SSRN: https://ssrn.com/abstract=3213954 or http://dx.doi.org/10.2139/ssrn.3213954
8 UK Government (1994). "Section 84, Criminal Justice and Public Order Act 1994". https ://www.legislation.gov.uk/ukpga/1994/33/section/84

be considered harassing, but also the willingness of law enforcement to proceed with a harassment case related to revenge pornography.

The issue of deterrent was also discussed with staff. The law enforcement response from a victim perspective has already been discussed and this was, once again, confirmed by staff. In their view, having legislation is not enough, the legislation needs to be in the public conscience but also needs awareness and effective application by law enforcement. A study in 2018[9] highlighted the problems the police face in addressing revenge pornography crimes, with a national police survey of almost 1000 officers showing less than 5% had received any training on either revenge pornography legislation or behaviours. There seems little point in enacting new legislation if those tasked with its enforcement have little awareness. Our work with the Revenge Porn Helpline, and their interactions with clients, very clearly shows that having legislation on the statute books is not enough to address a social problem – it requires enactment and awareness across the criminal justice system, not only to ensure offenders are punished but also to ensure victims are not exposed to further blame and judgement when they report crimes. A number of victims had commented on how their treatment by law enforcement had compounded their upset, particularly when met with judgemental and uncaring responses (such as "what do you want us to do about it?", "he can do what he likes with the pictures, he's done nothing wrong" or the perennial "if you hadn't sent him the pictures he wouldn't be able to share them"). In one case, a client of the helpline printed out the 2015 legislation and handed it to the police officer who saw nothing illegal about what her abuser had done. The officer in question said they were not aware of the legislation.

Moreover, there was some concern with the severity of sentencing for crimes that can leave victims suicidal, unemployed and suffering long-term mental health impacts. The maximum sentence set down in the England and Wales legislation is two years. However, it was the view of some staff that most sentencing is nowhere near the maximum in most cases. This is confirmed with an analysis of crime statistics reported by the Ministry of Justice to December 2018.[10]

Initial Application of the Legislation

To have any impact, new legislation needs to be well publicised and deployed, and it seems the CPS did just that.

The first prosecution took place almost immediately, with Jason Asagba pleading guilty to the offence on 16 May 2015. He was sentenced on 1 September

9 Bond, E., & Tyrrell, K. (2018). "Understanding revenge pornography: A national survey of police officers and staff in England and Wales". *Journal of Interpersonal Violence*, 0886260518760011.

10 UK Government (2019). "Criminal Justice System Statistics Quarterly: December 2018". https://www.gov.uk/government/statistics/criminal-justice-system-statistics-quarterly-december-2018

2016, receiving a six-month sentence, suspended for 18 months, 100 hours unpaid work and an order to pay £345 costs. Mr Asagba had texted explicit pictures of a 20-year-old woman to her family and shared them on her Facebook timeline, having hacked into her account. The pictures had been taken without her consent while she was asleep. A restraining order was also imposed banning Mr Asagba from contacting his victim or her family for four years. The facts of the Asagba case are sadly typical of a trend across a number of cases, with many defendants having hacked into their victim's social media accounts to post them on their own pages. In others, parody accounts had been set up. In the aftermath of his sentence, Director of Public Prosecutions, Alison Saunders, said that although it was too early to analyse trends, anecdotally, more cases of this kind were being referred by the police to the CPS since the legislation had come into force.

The first woman to be convicted was Paige Mitchell, who in September 2015 was given a six-week suspended sentence and ordered to pay £345 costs after uploading four explicit images of her girlfriend, complete with insulting captions. The posting was said to be in revenge for her girlfriend looking at other women.

With no sentencing guidance until 2018, courts were free to make their own judgements on the appropriateness of a sentence, but looking at cases that have been publicised in the media, overall, the level of sentence appears, in general, to be robust: most are suspended sentences of imprisonment, rather than community orders or lesser penalties, and there are several examples of immediate custodial sentences. In the absence of more explicit guidance, the courts appear to be following the Magistrates' sentencing guideline for offences of non-violent harassment (which carries the same maximum two-year sentence, and the most serious category of which involves "making personal photographs/sending offensive material" for which the suggested sentence is 18 weeks' imprisonment). This results in firm sentences overall: the s 33 offence carries the important distinction of not having to involve repetitious conduct and, unlike harassment cases, most of the reported cases seem to involve isolated instances. It would appear to be here, in the cases of the single but extremely damaging malicious disclosure, that the legislation is proving most effective.

The prosecution figures released by the CPS refer only to the number of prosecutions, not the number of cases referred to prosecutors. Freedom of Information (FOI) requests made by the BBC revealed that between April and December 2015, there had been 1160 reported incidents,[11] some alleged victims were as young as 11, with 61% of reported offences resulting in no action being taken. The main reasons cited were the lack of evidence or the victim withdrawing support for the action; 11% resulted in charges, 7% in a caution and 5% in a community resolution. At first look, this may suggest there is room for improve-

---

11 BBC News (2016). "Revenge porn: More than 200 Prosecuted Under New Law". *BBC News.* https://www.bbc.co.uk/news/uk-37278264

ment: domestic violence cases are now routinely approached as "victimless" prosecutions, and with most of these offences committed online, many ought to be
amenable to a similar approach. However, lack of consent is an essential element
of the offence which needs to be proved, and cases are likely to be few where that
can be established without direct evidence from the victim.

This early data on the nature of arrests and charges illustrated that the legislation was having an impact and being applied. However, it also showed some
problematic issues, such as the legislation being applied in the case of young
victims. If the victim of image-based abuse is 11, it seems wholly inappropriate
to apply this legislation rather than the Protection of Children Act 1978 (albeit
with the proviso that CPS guidance on prosecution would also depend on the
age of the victim).

At the time of writing (April 2020), since enactment, there have been
1324 recorded crimes entering the England and Wales Criminal Justice System.
Of those crimes, as reported in the Ministry of Justice statistics:

- 867 were proceeded against, resulting in 736 convictions
- Majority of sentencing did not fall beyond a year, with 119 receiving a sentence of six months or less. In total, 22 of those sentenced received a custodial sentence of more 12 months or more
- The average fine for offences was £287, and the average amount of compen-
  sation awarded was £213

Certainly, within the helpline staff, there is a view that the maximum sentence
needs to be increased to become an effective deterrent. One should note that in
the Scottish legislation, the maximum sentence is five years.

In July 2018, the Sentencing Council, as a result of consultation on the new
legislation (among others), produced its first set of sentencing guidance related
to the act,[12] which showed significant learning about the nature of the crime and
potential mitigation. Culpability hinges on the intention to cause distress, duration of abuse and sophistication of offence. Learning difficulties or mental capacity issues are listed as indicators of lower culpability. Harm categorisation lists
prolonged abuse and psychological harm as aspects, and aggravating factors were
wide-ranging, including offending while on bail, hostility related to protected
characteristics under the Equality Act 2010,[13] obstructing disclosure, aggrega-
tion with other domestic abuse factors or failing to comply with court orders.
Mitigating factors included remorse, good character, lack of maturity, mental
capacity and restitutive response. This has been welcomed by the helpline and

12 Sentencing Council (2018). "Intimidatory Offences - Definitive Guideline". https://ww
w.sentencingcouncil.org.uk/wp-content/uploads/Intimidatory-offences-definitive-guidel
ine-Web.pdf
13 UK Government (2010). "Equality Act 2010". http://www.legislation.gov.uk/ukpga
/2010/15/contents

will hopefully result in more consistent sentencing and a focus on victim impact. However, data to date is not sufficiently timely to be able to illustrate the impact of this guidance.

In further enumerating the impact of the new legislation, the Ministry of Justice figures, when explored in more detail, show that it is at least being applied in increasing numbers as the years progress. The overall breakdown of outcomes from those entering the justice system is detailed in Table 5.1.

The legislation is certainly being applied and resulting in prosecutions. In the majority of cases, it is being used against male abusers over the age of 20. However, there is also a sizable minority of female offenders being charged, although they are more likely to receive a caution. Males are far more likely to be convicted and sentenced, which would reflect that the majority of severe cases to date are against males. It is encouraging that the legislation is not being applied to minors in a significant number, something we have already discussed in the

Table 5.1 Ministry of Justice Charge Statistics against Section 33 of the Criminal Justice and Courts Act 2015

	2015	2016	2017	2018
All				
Cautions issued	74	147	141	95
Proceeded against	82	267	294	224
Convicted	64	228	261	183
Sentenced	63	228	251	183
Juvenile only				
Cautions issued	3	18	9	8
Proceeded against	1	6	8	4
Convicted	1	2	7	2
Sentenced	1	2	7	2
Juvenile and young adult[a]				
Cautions issued	22	48	42	28
Proceeded against	14	40	46	29
Convicted	10	32	41	18
Sentenced	10	32	38	18
Male				
Cautions issued	50	97	102	65
Proceeded against	74	227	254	202
Convicted	58	198	227	164
Sentenced	57	199	217	164
Female				
Cautions issued	19	48	38	26
Proceeded against	7	36	40	20
Convicted	5	29	34	18
Sentenced	5	28	34	19

Source: Ministry of Justice.
[a] *"Young adult" is defined as between the ages of 18 and 20.*

earlier chapters. CPS guidance also reiterates the appropriateness of using this legislation when offenders and victims are minors:

> Where images may have been taken when the victim was under 18, prosecutors should consider whether any offences under section 1 of the Protection of Children Act 1978 (taking, distributing, possessing or publishing indecent photographs of a child) or under section 160 of the Criminal Justice Act 1988 (possession of an indecent photograph of a child) have been committed. Further information is available in the legal guidance on Indecent Images of Children.

Teen Sexting and the Criminal Justice Process

However, care should be taken when considering any cases of "sexting" that involve images taken of persons under 18. Sexting commonly refers to the sharing of illicit images, videos or other content between two or more persons. Sexting can cover a broad range of activities, from the consensual sharing of an image between two children of a similar age in a relationship to instances of children being exploited, groomed and bullied into sharing images, which in turn may be shared with peers or adults without their consent.

However, the CPS refers to the public interest in pursuing this form of prosecution.

> Whilst it would not usually be in the public interest to prosecute the consensual sharing of an image between two children of a similar age in a relationship, a prosecution may be appropriate in other scenarios. In addition to the offences outlined above, consideration may be given to the offence of Causing or inciting a child to engage in sexual activity under section 8 (child under 13) or section 10 (child) of the Sexual Offences Act 2003 (SOA).

Nevertheless, there have been cases reported where children have ended up with police cautions for such behaviour where evidence of coercion or predation was lacking. If one refers to Ministry of Justice official statistics under section 1 of the Protection of Children Act, there is clear evidence that there has been a growth in those cautioned or proceeded against since 2008 until 2016, a time when teen sexting was on the rise (Table 5.2).

While this data cannot be interpreted to state all of these charges will have resulted from self-generation, it is safe to assume the growth in cautions and charges is, in part, as a result. However, increased awareness of the application of this (aged) legislation for a modern-day phenomenon has raised public concern. For example,[14] in one case, a 14-year-old boy who was involved in three

---

14 Ward, V. (2015). "Teenage Boy Added to Police Database for Sexting". *The Telegraph*. https ://www.telegraph.co.uk/news/uknews/crime/11840985/Teenage-boy-added-to-police-database-for-sexting.html

Table 5.2 Charges against s1 Protection of Children Act 1978 Where Accused Is Either a Minor or Young Adult (2008–2018)

	2008	2009	2010	2011	2012	2013	2014	2015	2016	2017	2018
Cautions issued	52	47	44	59	45	64	78	90	114	80	61
Proceeded against	39	41	41	40	34	38	49	54	61	53	42
Convicted	33	33	36	37	26	28	38	46	56	37	40
Sentenced	33	33	36	36	27	28	38	47	54	39	40

Source: Ministry of Justice.

"sexting" incidents at a school, sending pictures of his genitals via Snapchat and receiving an image of the recipient in return. In the first case, a police schools officer visited the school and told the boy to not do this again because it could be considered criminal. In two further cases, there was an exchange of images with someone else and, after falling out, he shared the image of the second recipient with a third party. While the police (the Greater Manchester force) did not arrest or charge the boy, they did file a crime report against his name under "obscene publications" for two of the later incidents. Therefore, should the boy be subject to criminal records checks in the future, it is possible this will return a recorded crime under "obscene publications". Once the boy turned 18, there was a judicial review launched at the request of the boy's mother against the Chief Constable of Greater Manchester Police, who has refused to remove this record from the boy who stated that she did not feel a moment of teenaged naivety should be held over him for his entire adult life.[15] However, the review against the chief constable was dismissed,[16] the police concern being that the boy was demonstrating an escalation of behaviours around images that meant the recording might be necessary for protecting the community should he continue such behaviours into adult life. Furthermore, the review was challenging the Chief Constable on human rights grounds, arguing that the boy's Article 6 rights (the right to a fair trial) had not been supported because he was in receipt of a crime report with no trial or hearing. However, this was dismissed because a crime report, while using language similar to a criminal record, is not, of itself, tantamount to a trial, therefore, article 6 does not apply.

A further claim was lodged under Article 8 (a right to respect for one's "private and family life, his home and his correspondence"). This was, again dismissed, because the view was held that crime recording was necessary for the public interest should behaviours continue to escalate.

Therefore, the boy remains with a crime report against his name that *could* be retrieved in the event of him obtaining employment in a job that requires a criminal record check.

While there is balance in the judicial review, and fair comment by police for the retention of the report, the irony of the case is that in response to cases such as the one above, and the resultant media commentary, in 2016, the College of Policing[17] issued its own guidance, which allows a sexting incident to be reported and recorded, without the child ending up with a criminal record. The recording of a crime as "outcome 21" to a "sexting" crime became official advice from the College of Policing in late 2016. An outcome 21 record states:

15 BBC (2017). "Mum Wins Legal Review Over Police Keeping Son's Naked Photo Detail". *BBC News.* https://www.bbc.co.uk/news/uk-england-manchester-41945498
16 Peel, N. (2018). "A Pattern of Behaviour". https://www.weightmans.com/insights/a-pattern-of-behaviour/
17 College of Policing (2016). "Police action in response to youth produced Sexual Imagery ('Sexting')". http://www.college.police.uk/News/College-news/Documents/Police_action_in_response_to_sexting_-_briefing_(003).pdf

Further investigation, resulting from the crime report, which could provide evidence sufficient to support formal action being taken against the suspect is not in the public interest – police decision.

The guidance made it clear that this recording could only be used in the event that there was no evidence of harmful or abusive intent and/or acts associated with the act of sharing the image:

> Outcome 21 may be considered the most appropriate resolution in youth produced sexual imagery cases where the making and sharing is considered non-abusive and there is **no evidence** of exploitation, grooming, profit motive, malicious intent (e.g. extensive or inappropriate sharing (e.g. uploading onto a pornographic website) or it being persistent behaviour. Where these factors are present, outcome 21 would not apply.

This development was viewed as a progressive step forwards in policing, while still being constrained by the limitations of the legislation. However, there were still anecdotal concerns expressed by schools we have visited around the country that while this recording option was available to police officers, its application was inconsistent across the country – some schools were aware of such recording, some were not, and many still had police talks to their students where the only advice was "don't send nudes, it's illegal".

As a result of these concerns, research was commissioned with which one of the authors (Phippen) of this text was involved. Drawing upon data from the analysis of Freedom of Information requests to all forces to determine the use of outcome 21 for teen sexting cases, alongside arrest data that might indicate how often the 1978 legislation was still being used, we can see a patchy and inconsistent picture across the country.

The data reported upon[18] suggested that there seems still be numerous arrests of minors for these activities and that new police powers that allow them to record a crime without it appearing formally on a young person's criminal record are being applied disproportionately and excessively by some forces.

The research was conducted using Freedom of Information requests to police forces expressed as:

- Please could you provide details of the number of arrests related to the taking, making or distribution of an indecent (or pseudo sexual) image of a child (home office code 86/2) where the suspect was under the age of 18 since December 2016.

18 Phippen, A., and Bond, E. (2019). "Police Response to Youth Offending Around the Generation and Distribution of Indecent Images of Children and its Implications". https://www.uos.ac.uk/sites/default/files/FOI-Report-Final-Outcome-21.pdf

- If you hold the information, please could you also provide details of the number of arrests related to the taking, making or distribution of an indecent (or pseudo sexual) image of a child (home office code 86/2) where the suspect was under the age of 14 since December 2016.
- Please could you provide the total number of crimes related to the taking, making or distribution of an indecent (or pseudo sexual) image of a child (home office code 86/2) where the suspect was under 18 that have been recorded as Outcome 21, since December 2016.
- If you hold the information, please could you also provide the total number of crimes related to the taking, making or distribution of an indecent (or pseudo sexual) image of a child (home office code 86/2) where the suspect was under the age of 14 that have been recorded as Outcome 21 since December 2016.

The request for under 14 data as well as minors (under 18) in general was to determine the level of potential criminalisation of younger teens and pre-teens using this legislation developed to protect children from exploitation by adults and whether outcome 21 was being applied in these cases.

It is acknowledged that that, as with any Freedom of Information request related to crime data held, the response will not allow the exploration of the context of activity leading to arrest, for example, differentiating between those who might have self-generated, those who might have shared self-generated images and those who might have accessed indecent images of minors online.

Breaking down responses per force, there is great variety in both arrest under the PCA 1978, and the application of outcome 21 recording, with some forces using this recording in far great quantities than arrests, particularly for those younger "offenders" (Table 5.3).

What is clear from these results is:

- Children and young people are still being arrested under this legislation
- Some forces have arrested minors under the age of 14
- Outcome 21 recording is being applied by most forces, in greatly varying volumes
- The number of outcome 21 recordings, in more cases, far exceeds the number of arrests (in some cases there is a tenfold difference)

If one returns to the Ministry of Justice official crime reporting, there is a clear tailing off of minors entering the criminal justice system under s1 PCA 1978 (Table 5.4).

And the responses to the FOI requests demonstrate that while charges may be reducing, outcome 21 is being applied in far higher numbers. While one may, and should, view this as positive for young people, one should remain mindful that while it is viewed as a "non-conviction", the wording of the police guidance states:

Table 5.3 Arrests and Outcome 21 Recording of Minors against Section 1 of the Protection of Children Act 1978 by Police Authority

	Arrests 14–17	Arrests <14	OC21 14–17	OC21 <14
Avon and Somerset Constabulary	8	0	85	70
Bedfordshire Police	2	0	67	29
Cambridgeshire Constabulary	10	0	17	34
Cheshire Constabulary	4	0	0	10
Cleveland Police	3	0	2	0
Derbyshire Constabulary	3	7	300	204
Devon and Cornwall Police	2	0	103	43
Dorset Police	2	0	103	43
Durham Constabulary	3	0	9	1
Gloucestershire Constabulary	6	1	78	31
Greater Manchester Police	6	3	414	495
Gwent Police	4	0	0	0
Hampshire Constabulary	15	1	2	0
Hertfordshire Constabulary	5	0	117	67
Kent Police	15	3	103	31
Leicestershire Police	8	0	38	90
Lincolnshire Police	7	0	171	117
Merseyside Police	6	0	80	42
Metropolitan Police Service	102	10	54	166
Norfolk Constabulary	14	0	75	60
North Yorkshire Police	18	2	0	2
South Yorkshire Police	0	0	0	2
Staffordshire Police	5	0	365	294
Suffolk Constabulary	17	1	99	67
Sussex Police	8	3	70	49
Thames Valley Police	16	1	257	227
Warwickshire Police	1	0	77	30
West Mercia Police	8	0	112	58
West Midlands Police	10	5	153	367
Wiltshire Police	7	1	0	0

Source: Phippen and Bond 2019.

The discretion on whether to disclose non-conviction information rests with each chief constable managing the process.

In other words, should a minor with an outcome 21 recording be in a position in later life that a DBS check (or whatever the future criminal record check might

Table 5.4 Charges against s1 Protection of Children Act 1978 Where Accused Is Either a Minor or Young Adult (2016–2018)

	2016	2017	2018
Cautions issued	114	80	61
Proceeded against	61	53	42
Convicted	56	37	40
Sentenced	54	39	40

Source: Ministry of Justice.

be) is needed, there is still a chance that this will still be disclosed. As can be seen with this data, major discrepancies show outcome 21 being applied differently across forces. Without published policy on how this discretion by chief constables is applied, a minor in one part of the country who is spoken to by the police as a result of a sexting activity might be treated differently to someone living under another police force location.

It might be assumed that outcome 21 is being applied in far more cases because of the belief that there is no lasting impact on the young person. This is not necessarily the case and the system risks a soft criminalisation of children who, prior to the inception of outcome 21, were more likely to have received a telling off and told to be more mindful in the future.

While there have been examples of law enforcement responses that have clearly been problematic in terms of victim support and knowledge of relevant legislation, there are also clear issues around training, resourcing and support. Having legislation is not sufficient, addressing the societal issues around revenge pornography and teen sexting requires buy-in from a number of stakeholders in victim protection, rather than hoping that, with the implementation of legislation, these issues will go away, because they will not. While the definition of well thought out legislation is a fundamental foundation of supporting victims and punishing those who wish to harm others in society, it needs to be understood by society as a whole, and those tasked with the enforcement of the law need to have sufficient training and resources to be able to do their job effectively. There is also a need for well thought out legislation. Having any legislation is not sufficient and, in some cases where older laws are applied to emergent social phenomena (such as teen sexting), the legislation can be damaging and increase harm to the victim.

The Tension Between the Law and Enforcement

By way of example, the following briefly considers a complimentary, but differing, piece of legislation, and the response to that legislation by a former police officer. The Serious Crime Act 2015 included a section (67) to close a gap in

the 2003 Sexual Offences Act around sexualised communication with a child.[19]
Specifically:

67 Sexual communication with a child

After section 15 of the Sexual Offences Act 2003 insert—
"15A Sexual communication with a child

(1) A person aged 18 or over (A) commits an offence if—
   (a) for the purpose of obtaining sexual gratification, A intentionally communicates with another person (B),
   (b) the communication is sexual or is intended to encourage B to make (whether to A or to another) a communication that is sexual, and
   (c) B is under 16 and A does not reasonably believe that B is 16 or over.
(2) For the purposes of this section, a communication is sexual if—
   (a) any part of it relates to sexual activity, or
   (b) a reasonable person would, in all the circumstances but regardless of any person's purpose, consider any part of the communication to be sexual;
   and in paragraph (a) 'sexual activity' means an activity that a reasonable person would, in all the circumstances but regardless of any person's purpose, consider to be sexual.
(3) A person guilty of an offence under this section is liable—
   (a) on summary conviction, to imprisonment for a term not exceeding 12 months or a fine or both;
   (b) on conviction on indictment, to imprisonment for a term not exceeding 2 years".

The new legislation attracted significant press attention because, while it was written into law in 2015, it did not become enacted until 2017, as a result in part to the NSPCC's "Flaw in the Law" campaign.[20]

While the enactment was generally welcomed, at the same time, a former detective inspector posted a blog about the new legislation which captures the reality faced by law enforcement with this sort of legislation, which is a useful juxtaposition when considering legislation specific to revenge pornography and teen sexting:

19 UK Government (2015). "Serious Crime Act 2015". https://www.legislation.gov.uk/ukpga/2015/9/section/67/enacted
20 NSPCC (2017). "Flaw in the Law". https://www.nspcc.org.uk/what-we-do/campaigns/flaw-law/

Child "A" is on his or her Facebook Account (or any medium, including text messaging). The child "befriends" "B" and "B" uses explicit sexual language. Child "A", unlike the majority of children who will not report this type of incident, speak to his/her parents. They in turn quite correctly make a report to the police. This then should start off a sequence of events. Firstly the child will require an Achieving Best Evidence interview to establish the full facts (finding facilities and trained staff to resource this is often problematic). The computer or other device will then be seized to join the already lengthy queue for forensic examination, currently most Forces, giving the best case scenario have a backlog of around six months. In order to resolve the location of the suspect an officer will have to submit a RIPA application so the provider will disclose the address of their customer. The cost of this on average is around £70 per check (yes the industry are making money out of this). As is the case in the majority of similar incidents online the suspect is unlikely to … reside in the same Force area as the victim. The next challenge is to send a package to that other Force and try and convince them that this particular case needs attention over their own heavy workloads. In our case we assume the police have identified the suspect and have made a swift arrest. The suspect will now be interviewed… as I see it the prosecution must prove beyond all reasonable doubt that the suspect sent the communication "for the purpose of obtaining sexual gratification". Without evidence of such activity in the communication, and if there is this will be easier to prove, the suspect for there to be a successful prosecution will have to admit the reason was for the purpose of sexual gratification in his or her police interview. The majority of suspects will of course be legally represented and, I would suggest the solicitor would either cause the suspect to say there was no gratification or make no comment. Making such a comment or remaining silent would probably be interpreted by an already overstretched CPS as not reaching the threshold for there to be a successful prosecution.[21]

The post makes a number of valid concerns for law enforcement tasked with enforcing legislation:

1. Initial resourcing to collect evidence
2. Digital forensics and the dearth of resourcing in that area
3. The cost of accessing data
4. Inter-force cooperation
5. Proof of sexual gratification
6. Willingness of CPS to proceed

---

21 Snell, S. (2017). "These views are my own and not reflective of". http://www.safeguard ingassociatesforexcellence.co.uk/wp-content/uploads/2017/03/Article-Comm-with-Ch ild-.pdf

All of these are valid concerns and reflect law enforcement's stretched resources, even if knowledge of all of the appropriate legislation is sound.

It can be seen that there is a continual reactive, and arguably *hyperactive*, legislative response to these problems, which can lead to the criminal justice system, and the wider safeguarding workforce, trying to catch up with the development of the statute.

Upskirting – The Next Image-Based Abuse Legal Conundrum?

In April 2019, upskirting became illegal in England and Wales for the first time under the Voyeurism (Offences) Act 2019 (s67A 1 and 2).[22] It is worth reflecting on the emergent legislation to see what things have progressed from the Criminal Justice and Courts Act 2015) and whether there is consistency in the legislative developments.

Upskirting, the practice of covertly photographing a person's genital or anal region, often to distribute the footage online,[23] so named because this occurs commonly with the placement of a mobile phone beneath a victim's skirt. Its emergence as an antisocial practice is a straightforward one – with the widespread adoption of mobile devices, most of which contain cameras, this unpleasant practice is more straightforward to do than it would have been when cameras were more cumbersome devices. One of the key themes of this text to date is that legislation struggles to keep up with society to protect victims from emergent abusive methods, particularly when applied through the use of disruptive technology, and when the focus of the debate is to "stop" the practice, rather than address route causes, in the legislation.

In the case of upskirting, as a result of a dearth of protection for victims, one can see the emergence of legitimisation ("this is something that the press have been doing for years", "if they don't want pictures taken they shouldn't wear short skirts", "its only feminists who don't think it's funny") and passive acceptance by victims ("no-one will do anything to stop it", "what is the point in complaining?") who either do not believe they have a right to protection or don't feel there is any point in making a complaint. There are clear parallels here with our empirical work with both teen sexting and revenge pornography victims. As already discussed when exploring the Revenge Porn Helpline casebook, many victims will say it's their own fault and they didn't think anyone would take them seriously, even when subjected to serious subsequent coercion or exploitation as a result of an intimate image being shared or a threat to share. Equally, when

22 Ibid.
23 Thompson C (2016). "Skirting around the issue paper: Problematizing the representation of upskirting in Australian media and political discourses". *Violence Against Women*. doi: 10.1177/1077801219870606

speaking to and observing bystanders who blame the victim for placing themselves in a vulnerable position in the first place, this view is reinforced.

The growing concern about upskirting, alongside other technologically mediated sexual misdemeanours and offences, has also attracted academic discourse,[24] which has led to calls for UK legislation to catch up with other jurisdictions and bring out a law that will provide a means to prosecute those conducting such practices.[25] In some jurisdictions, there has been "upskirting" legislation for over ten years, for example, in the Australian state of Victoria.[26] Yet it has only been recently that legislation for England and Wales has been enacted.[27]

By way of coincidence with the PCA 1978, the introduction of the legislation was not initiated by the government, but by the concerns of an individual member of parliament.

The Liberal Democrat MP Wera Hobhouse proposed a Private Members Bill to the House of Commons that moved to debate in June 2018. However, while it was granted a debate, it attracted attention due to an objection by the Conservative MP Sir Christopher Chope. He blocked the debate on a parliamentary technicality. He stated that he objected on a point of principle – the bill should not be introduced through a private member but by government, such that it could be given sufficient time to be properly debated.

Clearly, upskirting is a growing issue. In our own discussions in schools and universities, we can see that it is both a problematic behaviour and also one where victims are almost accepting of harassment – the expectation being that it will happen and you just have to put up with it. There are comments such as "if I hadn't worn a skirt, I guess they wouldn't have been able to do this" or "it's just something lads do". On the side of those taking the images, the view is rarely that this is a problematic thing to do – it's just "a bit of fun" or, the perennial justification – "banter".

Given this is new legislation that has occurred since the Criminal Justice and Courts Act 2015, with its attempt to tackle image-based abuse with clear and effective legislation, it should be hoped that some of the issues around this legislation (for example, proof of gratification or harm and threat) might be strengthened. We have discussed, over the last three chapters, the flaws in legislation in

24 Butler, D., Kift, S., and Campbell, M. (2009). "Cyber bullying in schools and the law: Is there an effective means of addressing the power imbalance". *eLaw Journal*, *16*, 84.

25 McGlynn, C., and Rackley, E. (2017). "Why 'upskirting' needs to be made a sex crime". *The conversation*. https://theconversation.com/why-upskirting-needs-to-be-made-a-sex-crime-82357

26 Victoria State Government 2017. Summary Offences Amendment (Upskirting) Act 2007. http://www.legislation.vic.gov.au/Domino/Web_Notes/LDMS/PubStatbook.nsf/f93 2b66241ecf1b7ca256e92000e23be/915C6CEDFEA5FEEFCA25736100205870/$F ILE/07-049a.pdf

27 UK Government (2019). Voyeurism (Offences) Act 2019. http://www.legislation.gov.uk/ukpga/2019/2/section/1/enacted

these areas and we would have hoped that lessons could have been learned from previous legislation that would mean flaws could be addressed.

In tackling the problem, Ms Hobhouse's Private Member's Bill proposed to extend the Sexual Offences Act 2003 to incorporate further voyeuristic elements that incorporate upskirting behaviours.

There are both encouraging and concerning aspects of the legislation. On the one hand, it is good to see the consideration of a third party in the act – if someone is taking an image or video to share with someone else. It also makes clear with the legislation that intent is also unlawful, there does not have to be an image capture or broadcast for prosecution to take place:

(1) A person (A) commits an offence if—
  (a) A operates equipment beneath the clothing of another person (B),
  (b) A does so with the intention of enabling A or another person (C), for a purpose mentioned in subsection (3), to observe—
    (i) B's genitals or buttocks (whether exposed or covered with underwear), or
    (ii) the underwear covering B's genitals or buttocks,
    in circumstances where the genitals, buttocks or underwear would not otherwise be visible, and
  (c) A does so—
    (i) without B's consent, and
    (ii) without reasonably believing that B consents.
(2) A person (A) commits an offence if—
  (a) A records an image beneath the clothing of another person (B),
  (b) the image is of—
    (i) B's genitals or buttocks (whether exposed or covered with underwear), or
    (ii) (ii)the underwear covering B's genitals or buttocks,
    in circumstances where the genitals, buttocks or underwear would not otherwise be visible,
  (c) A does so with the intention that A or another person (C) will look at the image for a purpose mentioned in subsection (3), and
  (d) A does so—
    (i) without B's consent, and
    (ii) without reasonably believing that B consents.

Equally, the legislation clearly defines the illegality of the act of actually capturing an image:

A person ("A") commits an offence if A—

(a) without another person ("B") consenting, and 15
(b) without any reasonable belief that B consents,

records an image beneath B's clothing of B's genitals or buttocks (whether exposed or covered with underwear) or the underwear covering B's genitals or buttocks, in circumstances where the genitals, buttocks or underwear would not otherwise be visible, with the intention that A or another person ("C"), for a purpose mentioned in subsection (3), will look at the image.

It is also encouraging to see it clearly set out that consent is central to the offence, or reasonable assumption of consent – it is up to the offender to address the issue of consent, it is no defence to say consent was implied.

It is equally welcome that the legislation does not end with the taking of static images, as there is some effort to future proof the legislation and ensure that technical arguments about the nature of the capture (e.g. the taker made a video rather than an image) cannot be argued. Moreover, other techniques that are just becoming mainstream such as live streaming would also be covered.

However, perhaps the first area of concern lies in with the motivational definition once more:

(3) The purposes referred to in subsections (1) and (2) are—

(a) obtaining sexual gratification (whether for A or C);
(b) humiliating, alarming or distressing B.

The onus for prosecution once again lies on proof of intention to cause harm to the victim or for sexual gratification. This focus is concerning because both are difficult to categorically prove. On the one hand, this is a development from the revenge pornography legislation, in that intent to obtain gratification does at least show a sexual motivation, and therefore, means the law can be considered sexual with all of the benefits that afford the victim, such as anonymity. However, this provides an immediate and straightforward defence for the offender – they did this as a joke, they did not mean any harm, they are sorry if offence or upset was caused and so forth.

The question for this advice, and also any legislation that would require interpretation by law enforcement or the criminal justice process is "how can we interpret the intentions of the abuser/offender?"

Regardless of intention to cause harm or sexual gratification, if the victim feels harmed, would that be a more effective measure of the impact of the behaviour? If the victim says that as a result of this action, they felt harassed, violated or abused, should the intention, or reported intention, of the abuser take precedent? One might question why anyone would wish to place a mobile phone under the skirt of a victim and take an image in a manner that is anything other than abusively or sexually motivated. Similar wording appears in both English/Welsh Criminal Justice and Courts Act 2015 and Scottish (Abusive Behaviour and Sexual Harm Act) legislation, which, as already discussed, may be a contributing factor to the low proportion of cases moving to prosecution.

Moreover, this does now place two similar offences – revenge pornography and upskirting, at odds with each other. The arguments for not allowing the non-consensual sharing of intimate images to be a sexual crime discussed in the previous chapter no longer stand.

While the upskirting legislation specifically states in subsection 3(a) of "obtaining sexual gratification", we would argue that both pieces of legislation address the non-consensual sharing of intimate images, and are now in conflict as one is considered a sexual crime where the other is not. Again, the difference that it is possible to view the images in a "revenge pornography" scenario as self-generated, and therefore, there might be some fault on the part of the victim is a concern and potentially introduces revictimisation. The work with the Revenge Porn Helpline reveals that there are many occurrences where the images/videos themselves are not taken consensually in the first place (and for the sexual gratification of those taking the images) – there are many cases where covert image capture had taken place and parallels between the two forms of abuse.

However, perhaps the biggest concern from this proposed legislation is the lack of consideration of the age of the abuser and victim. Media discourse can play a distorting role when it applies the revenge pornography narrative to youth offenders and victims. There should be a clear distinction – those past the age of majority should be subjected to legislation related to the non-consensual sharing of images (s33 Courts and Serious Crime Act 2015), for minors, it is the manufacture and distribution of indecent images of a minor (s1 Sexual Offences Act 1978).

Within the new upskirting legislation, while there is some provision in the act to acknowledge the age of the offender, this related mainly to the notification requirements in the Sexual Offences Act. Within the new legislation, it sets out that the notification conditions for a minor are only met if the sentencing is for more than 12 months – therefore, an offender under the age of 18 for whom a significant sentence has been applied.

A concern with the application of the upskirting legislation to minor-on-minor incidents is the potentially disproportionate impact of the punishment. On the one hand, a clear message needs to be sent to potential victims that upskirting is unacceptable and you should not have to expect to put up with those behaviours. Yet, we also need to acknowledge that a 12-year-old might engage with this practice because they have not received any education on consent, respect and boundaries that has pointed out the severity or offensiveness of the act. There is a clear applicability of outcome 21 guidance to these crimes if they were committed peer on peer in the school setting (or even out of the school setting, where perpetrated by minors).

With the upskirting legislation surely there was an opportunity to embed this in the legislation, rather than hope for it to be addressed in subsequent guidance some years after enactment? This was developed in 2018/19, after many years of legal debate around the application of the law around the taking of indecent images by minors and non-consensual sharing. It was an opportunity to have learned from the experiences of the enactment of similar legislation to place this nuance from the outset, rather than retroactively. However, this does not seem to have been borne out in the new legislation.

One might imagine a scenario where that 12-year old-child who has upskirted is brought into the headteacher's office to be warned they might end up with a custodial sentence for doing something they weren't even aware was socially unacceptable, let alone illegal. We would have hoped the legislation could differentiate between this scenario and that of an adult taking an image of a stranger in the street. Yet the current proposed legislation does not have provision for this. We would have hoped through debate more subtlety could be introduced, in the rush to get this into law to avoid a potentially negative public reaction to the blocking of the bill by Sir Christopher Chope, this was not the case, even though it was debated:

Lord Keen of Elie (Con)[28]

Certainly, we must be careful not to overcriminalise children. But we believe that the Bill is correct and proportionate in how it deals with those under the age of 18 who commit this offence for reasons of sexual gratification. The sentencing threshold will mean that only the most serious offenders under 18, who also have a sexual motive, are made subject to notification requirements.

Indeed, if one considers the most up-to-date guidance on safeguarding to schools in England and Wales, the Keeping Children Safe in Education 2019 Update,[29] there is a single mention of upskirting, which is to remind professionals that it is now a criminal offence:

113 "Upskirting" typically involves taking a picture under a person's clothing without them knowing, with the intention of viewing their genitals or buttocks to obtain sexual gratification, or cause the victim humiliation, distress or alarm. It is now a criminal offence.

Therefore, the message to schools is that this is a criminal offence. In an alarming sense of déjà vu, this messaging, we might hypothesise, will now be used to threaten minors who have engaged in such practices, and assemblies will make it clear that engaging in such acts can result in prosecution. While one might argue they should not, as discussed in Chapter 2, a dearth of education around these sorts of behaviours is not helpful. One cannot assume minors will learn about the unacceptability of these behaviours through some sort of social osmosis – they are

28 Hansard (2018). "22nd October 2018. Volume 793, Column 785". http://bit.ly/2tDlUC7
29 UK Government (2019). "Keeping Children Safe in Education 2019 Update". https://
    assets.publishing.service.gov.uk/government/uploads/system/uploads/attachment_data/
    file/835733/Keeping_children_safe_in_education_2019.pdf

calling out for education and we are not providing it. In what we might assume is an attempt to tackle this in the early stages of enactment, the Crown Prosecution Service have put out guidance to remind those within the criminal justice system about public interest:[30]

> When determining if a charge under this legislation is appropriate prosecutors need to consider all the circumstances surrounding the offence. Specifically for this offence, particularly in relation to youths, consideration may need to be given as to whether this is a pattern of behaviour towards this or other victims, is sexually motivated, or whether it is an isolated incident or practical "joke".

Is Legislation Enough?

In this analysis, concerns have been raised around the effectiveness of legislation in protecting victims of technologically facilitated sexual crimes (or even that the legislation is incorrectly classified as communications crimes), and that there seems to be little attempt to be more progressive or victim focused with emerging legislation. The focus, as ever, seems to be on preventing the act, rather than challenging the culture that facilitates such approaches. What is clear from our communications with stakeholders (such as the Revenge Porn Helpline, but also others such as school teachers and senior leaders) is there is a view that education is an essential part of building knowledge and awareness of the impact of non-consensual sharing on victims and developing cultural change that moves our focus from victim blaming to "sharer blaming". There is also a need for education that makes people aware of what can be done to tackle non-consensual sharing, such a reporting and takedown notices. Staff at the Revenge Porn Helpline view this as something that needs to be tackled by a wide range of stakeholders, including general practitioners, mental health professions, domestic violence services, counselling professionals, universities and employers. And, as already discussed, there is an urgent need to challenge broad cultural norms among law enforcement and challenge apathy towards domestic abuse-related crime.

The role of the employer in supporting victims cannot be underestimated. The distressing case of a teacher who discovered that an ex-partner had posted a video of her (non-consensually filmed in the first place) when she was a minor onto Pornhub, which was subsequently discovered by students at her school, has already been discussed. In this case, her employer, rather than supporting her, decided to suspend her, therefore, further compounding the impact of the crime on the victim. While, due to the nature of the content, the takedown was straightforward (showing at least some level of responsibility from one stakeholder), the response of the employer seems to further exacerbate victim blaming.

---

30 Crown Prosecution Service (2019). "Voyeurism". https://www.cps.gov.uk/legal-guidance/voyeurism

There also needs to be wider cultural change around the judgement of victims in non-consensual sharing cases. We have already used media reporting, and subsequent public commentary, to illustrate this point around Marines United and the case of Kira Martin in Chapter 3.

If society as a whole does not take the non-consensual sharing of images, and its impact on victims, seriously (or even tries to explore ways in which victim blaming can be monetised), one cannot hope that the criminal justice system will be effective. Education is explored in far more detail in Chapter 7. One thing that arose from discussions with helpline staff were concerns about the dearth of education around the broader issues of the non-consensual sharing of images in schools, with any wider public education being virtually non-existent. The experiences of helpline staff were similar to our own – the majority of education is simply "don't do it, it's illegal". Client statements from the helpline have shown that these educational messages are following victims into adulthood. Many clients will say things like:

It was my own fault for taking the images in the first place.
I know now it's online, I cannot do anything about it.
I should have thought about the consequences before I shared them.

Clearly illustrating the impact of an educative approach that considers punitive action to be the best approach to prevention is something where the impact lasts well into adulthood. The lack of education that focused on abuse and harm has produced a generation that will still see the fault lying with the victim and those choosing to share images will not believe that they are doing anything wrong.

Helpline staff also felt that with the societal focus on the act, wider public understanding (for example, in the public health sphere) was also lacking, to the point where general practitioners and mental health professionals were not aware of the impact of non-consensual sharing on a victim's mental health, and therefore, were not equipped to help them effectively.

In this chapter, we have reviewed the effectiveness of legislation against empirical evidence and further analysis of the legal discourse and highlighted that, when tackling these emerging social issues, legislation struggles to be effective in isolation, particularly when there is a digital dimension. Legislation can only exist to punish abusers and protect victims; it cannot prevent acts in the first place. Throughout this discussion, we have returned to the fundamental concern that a single stakeholder cannot tackle these problems on their own, whether that stakeholder is the criminal justice system, law enforcement, education or service providers. All have a role to play, and all should be complementary. A lot of our evidence base explores the social legitimisation of sending "nudes" and the lack of concern around non-consensual sharing. If sharing and redistribution is a regular part of life for a significant number of teens, and also the adult population, will we ever, as a society, be able to recognise such behaviours as unacceptable and reinforce the rights of victims for protection under the law? In drawing this text to a close, we will consider the wider stakeholder community, with a focus on the role education *might* play in changing social attitudes and providing better support for victims, and potential abusers.

However, prior to a discussion around education, Chapter 6 will explore the frequent focus of public and political ire – the service providers, and argue that while technology might facilitate non-consensual sharing (and the production of the imagery in the first place), technology cannot prevent it and the service provider cannot be the sole responsible party in this wider stakeholder perspective.

6 Third-Party Responsibilities

The role of service providers, or third parties, in addressing the issues of image-based abuse and the non-consensual sharing of explicit images forms a subset of the wider political debate around the need for technology providers to "do more" in addressing online harms.

The Online Harms White Paper[1] that has already been discussed went to great lengths to talk about the "Duty of Care" service providers have when addressing online harms.

There is much made in the paper around the expectation of a "Duty of Care" for digital companies who might fall under the gaze of the new regulator:

> The government will establish a new statutory duty of care to make companies take more responsibility for the safety of their users and tackle harm caused by content or activity on their services.

However, what is lacking, as with a lot of the paper, given that its stated aim is legislative intent, and something that is reflected in digital policy in general, is detail about what this duty of care might look like and how it can be assessed. There is a claim that duty of care is important, and a regulator would ensure it was happening, but the detail on what it might be, and how it might be monitored, is less forthcoming.

There certainly seems to be little attempt to define or delineate whether this aligns with the broader legal concept of duty of care and its relationship with the tort of negligence. One might ask whether the duty of care in the white paper is being defined as a form of negligence, and therefore, a concept that can be unpinned with some case law to help said regulator make judgements on whether a service provider is negligent. At least in such cases, a service provider might be able to demonstrate due diligence or protect itself from vexatious claims of harm. However, legal negligence is certainly not, of itself, straightforward and is the

---

1 UK Government (2019). "Online Harms White Paper". https://assets.publishing.service.gov.uk/government/uploads/system/uploads/attachment_data/file/793360/Online_Harms_White_Paper.pdf

subject of much legal debate. There is general agreement that the evolution of the concept of negligence and the associated case law has not made our fundamental understanding of what negligence "is" any clearer, as rather beautifully expressed in "Markesinis and Deakin's Tort Law":[2]

> The experience of the last thirty years or so if anything, suggests a dialectical process of evolution with many, often inexplicable, tergiversations.

Given the language used, albeit without effective clarification, if the government is introducing failure to protect from online harm as another form of negligence for which one might make a civil claim, one might expect a level of detail in proposed legislation such that companies might understand the incoming legislative requirements on their content monitoring. Technological intervention is not something that can be developed overnight, and guidance at this stage would be welcome, particularly if a lack of compliance might leave service providers liable. One might wish to avoid political situations, such as the recent age verification debacle related to section 3 of the Digital Economy Act,[3] where companies who provided access to pornography were told that legislation was put in place such that they had to provide a strong method of preventing access to their sites by minors.[4] As one might expect, this triggered many developments within the service provider environment to ensure companies were compliant with legislation and not be found negligent. However, in the aftermath of the Online Harms White Paper, two years after the ascent of the legislation, it was announced that section 3 of the act would not be enacted.[5] It should be no surprise that at the time of writing, a number of service providers have launched a legal challenge against the government for "abuse of power"[6] where they are seeking £3m in damages and loss of earnings, based upon the considerable effort they had already invested in the development of solutions to this legislatively imposed technical measure. One would have hoped, therefore, that clarity would be defined around what the service provider duty of care looked like.

2 Deakin, Simon F., and Johnston, Angus C., and Markesinis, Basil S. (2012)." Markesinis & Deakin's Tort Law, 7th edition". Oxford University Press, p. 99.
3 UK Government (2017). "The Digital Economy Act 2017". http://www.legislation.gov.uk/ukpga/2017/30/contents/enacted
4 Department for Culture, Media and Sport (2017). "Digital Economy Bill Factsheet – Age Verification for Online Pornography (clauses 15–25)" https://assets.publishing.service.gov.uk/government/uploads/system/uploads/attachment_data/file/535010/6._Age_Verification_Fact_Sheet.pdf
5 Department of Digital, Culture, Media and Sport (2019). "ONLINE HARMS: Written statement – HCWS13". https://www.parliament.uk/business/publications/written-questions-answers-statements/written-statement/Commons/2019-10-16/HCWS13/
6 Wright (2020). "Tech companies Launch Legal Action to force Government to bring in under 18s Porn Ban". https://www.telegraph.co.uk/news/2020/01/16/tech-companies-launch-legal-action-force-government-bring-18s/

However, the only message they have from the white paper so far is "do more". What is more of a concern is the enforcement proposed extends beyond illegal to "harmful" content, even though the paper fails to define an exhaustive list of harmful content or even differentiates between harmful and illegal, thus failing to acknowledge the basic conceptual problem of the difference between harm and crime, and inadequately defining what the threshold is for constituting harm.

Which returns to a central argument in this problematic nature of these prohibitive approaches – it is not acknowledging the complexities of each of these issues, it is simply intended to tell companies that they have to "sort it out" or they risk their websites being blocked in the UK. Providers have two possible approaches to tackling harms on their services – either technical intervention or the provision of reactive and responsive reporting routes in the event of abuse or the discovery of harmful content being made.

This is a worrying development for competition, freedom of expression and even net neutrality. Should a regulator in the UK have the power to prevent the business practices of an organisation based upon their interpretation of what is "harmful" or "unacceptable" and whether the company have been sufficiently proactive? What is sufficiently proactive, or how does one demonstrate due diligence in the face of weakly defined expectations?

When it comes specifically to image-based abuse, the extent of service provider responsibility is complex – reporting and takedowns need to be clear, transparent and responsive, but given the difference in distribution platforms (for example, peer to peer, mobile, social media, "specialist" shaming websites and real-time distribution such as streaming video) this is sometimes not as simple as policymakers suggest. This chapter will explore these differences and challenges, and consider areas of good and less effective practice using two specific examples of attempts to place service providers at the heart of protection around image-based abuse that have arisen as a result of policy pressure that occurred prior to the Online Harms White Paper. The chapter will also explore why these approaches are doomed to fail and why there is an expectation of a response on the part of the service provider.

The Role of Stakeholders In Image-Based Abuse

However, the wider issues around stakeholder engagement show that the onus should not entirely be placed upon the service provider, and perhaps explains a little regarding why a service provider cannot address victim impact in the same way other stakeholders might. Even though many of the stakeholders in this area talk about responsibility, there is little evidence of this taking root in reality. Which does pose the question:

Why is the stakeholder space in this area so distorted when it comes to responsibility?

The discourse around this stakeholder discussion is a valid one to explore. It highlights the complexities of being a service provider with massive consumer bases and complex functionalities, while perhaps distracting from the roles of other stakeholders in this space. Even the concept of "service provider" is complicated in this area. As already discussed when relating this concept to image-based abuse, a service provider may be an entity that provides the means to create the image (device providers), distribute the image over mobile networks (telephony providers), distribute over IP-based networks (app and internet service providers), further post and share images (forum providers, website operators and social media providers) or increasingly those who provide the means to generate and distribute content in real time (live streaming providers).

However, all of these different stakeholders are often discussed as a single entity – the "service provider", even though their place in the technology stack, the functionality they provide or the means by which they can tackle the content distribution differs greatly. For example, a mobile operator might provide the means to distribute content across their network, but does that mean they should be responsible for the examination of all content within their network? While we will pick up on this "responsibility" in far more detail later in the chapter, it is worth pausing for a moment to reflect on this. While the focus of concern, in terms of risk and harm, is on the distribution of images, can one restrict the responsibility of the telephony provider to "just" look at images? If policymakers are saying that service providers have a responsibility to ascertain whether an image is harmful or unlawful, why would that expectation not extend to messages? Or perhaps even voice calls? As ever in this space, the question "just because technically it is possible, should we expect this?" needs to be asked. Would society be happy with private sector organisations accessing and vetting our communications in order to ensure "child safety" or reduce risk for the adult population?

If the reliance lies almost entirely on the role of a single stakeholder – the service provider – what will inevitably result is an error-prone and overzealous blocking approach. Content moderation is undoubtedly a complex thing to do – even after almost 20 years of filtering in schools, with conservative blocking de rigueur, harmful content can still, occasionally, get through, while overblocking is part of school life. In more recent times, the UK Government's Department for Education has acknowledged this with its most recent safeguarding guidance[7] using the term "appropriate" blocking, while stressing the need to "*be careful that 'overblocking' does not lead to unreasonable restrictions as to what children can be taught with regards to online teaching and safeguarding*". However, what blocking is deemed "appropriate" is not defined in the documentation and while guidance has been offered to schools,[8] even this guidance is non-prescriptive and

---

7 UK Government (2019). "Keeping Children Safe in Education 2019 Update". https://assets.publishing.service.gov.uk/government/uploads/system/uploads/attachment_data/file/835733/Keeping_children_safe_in_education_2019.pdf
8 UK Safer Internet Centre (2018). "Appropriate Filtering and Monitoring". https://www.saferinternet.org.uk/advice-centre/teachers-and-school-staff/appropriate-filtering-and-monitoring

certainly not tied to a legislative framework, leaving schools on their own to decide what, in fulfilling their statutory duties, is "appropriate".

The Technology to Sort it Out

There is a fundamental problem with moderation for algorithms, which has been discussed in depth elsewhere.[9] For the sake of this discussion, we will not go into as much detail but explore the salient points. Algorithmic intervention will always be rule, not principle, based. Even with textual analysis of abuse words used to construct a hateful or illegal statement can equally be used to create something innocuous. Therefore, judgement and interpretation are needed on any piece of content being analysed. Algorithms are hard-wired to their rule base and will miss nuance that can come from cultural or contextual meaning embedded in a post and while, through machine learning, algorithms can "learn" context, it is only ever a simulate of subjectivity, something based entirely on symbolic data.

Clearly, there are issues with a private sector organisation providing an online platform for over two billion people and whose business model provides an opaque and arguably inconsistent set of guidelines in order to moderate that content. However, perhaps more concerning is the willingness of governments to use this unease to justify increasingly strong powers to either exert pressure on the providers to "do more" to ensure hate speech (which can be defined against the Equalities Act 2010[10]), intimate content (less straightforward to define in law) or abuse (even more difficult to define in law) is not manifested on their platforms. If such powers result in platform providers being viewed as publishers, the potential ramifications are widespread. Clearly, social media providers and other online platforms that provide a voice for those whose views are, at best, unpalatable are an easy and visible target for stakeholder responsibility in this area. However, there is a strong risk that the visibility of the moral outrage around unpalatable comments being posted on these sites results in opportunities for governments to deflect from their own responsibilities while imposing disproportionate powers over free speech in an area where they know legislation would be unpalatable.

Moving more specifically to issues around sexting and revenge pornography, similar attempts have also been levelled in the area of mobile technology leading into issues around sexting and pornography.

This has long been endemic in the child online safety arena[11] and focuses on a fundamental challenge in addressing these social problems – prohibition is always viewed as more favourable than intervention or empowerment, and pro-

9 Phippen, A., and Brennan, M. (2019). "Child Protection and Safeguarding Technologies – Appropriate or Excessive 'Solutions' to Social Problems?". Routledge.

10 UK Government (2010). "Equality Act 2010". http://www.legislation.gov.uk/ukpga /2010/15/contents

11 Phippen, A. (2016). "Children's Online Behaviour and Safety: Policy and Rights Challenges". Palgrave.

hibition is generally viewed as something that can be achieved through technology. One might argue that this is an easier pitch to sell – "let's stop this" is a far more palatable headline than a more complex argument for a multi-stakeholder preventative approach that accepts these things are going to happen and aims to understand the impact and develop strategies to address it. However, one might argue that such a focus places too much emphasis on the responsibilities of one stakeholder while ignoring the role others might play. Certainly, the service/technology/platform provider has responsibilities – for example, providing routes for reporting, showing response to reports and defining clear acceptable use and terms and conditions. However, the extent to which a service provider can eliminate risk completely from their platforms, and proactively tackle any potential offending, reflects perhaps the lack of understanding of the nature of these platforms by other stakeholders and a willingness to deflect from the responsibility of others.

However, as fallout from these technical claims and the belief that technology can solve these "technical" issues, and as a result of safeguarding concerns and stakeholder blame deflection, there is an increasing marketplace for "safeguarding" software that aims to reassure parents and other adults with a duty of care that their children are prevented from engaging in the exchange of intimate, self-generated images. While some will use a simple sharing model – for example, sending any image sent from the child's phone to the parent's phone, others claim advanced image recognition capabilities, and the ability to reliably identify everything from indecency to self-harm. Several products offer a range of functionalities, such as alerting the parent when such an image is generated, forwarding the image to the parent or posting a warning on the child's phone about a suspect image.

Image recognition as an algorithm is notoriously complex. In a recent study of the more widely used image recognition engines,[12] using a small (2000) set of general images which algorithms were tasked with categorising (charts, landscapes, people and products), the most accurate algorithm was incorrect in over one in ten cases. If we were to take a more complex image set with more complicated parameters (such as "is this image a self-produced indecent image of a minor"), one might expect the recognition rate to drop significantly. We would, therefore, be concerned if such technologies were viewed as a "solution" for the problems arising from the generation and sharing of sexual images of minors. If a parent believed that installing an app of their child's phone will ensure they can't engage with practices such as sexting, again, this may result in a failure to more effectively address the root causes of such behaviours.

Similar policy suggestions have arisen in attempts to tackle teen sexting. In one case, from a government minister giving evidence to a select committee hearing. In November 2016, Jeremy Hunt, the UK Health Secretary, gave

12 Enge (2019). "Who Has the Best Image Recognition Engine?". https://www.perficientdigital.com/insights/our-research/image-recognition-accuracy-study

evidence to the Commons Health Committee's investigation into suicide prevention,[13] which raised concerns about the impact of technologically facilitated social behaviours on children's mental health and wellbeing. This is an admirable goal, and one that, at least on the face of it, attempted to move the debate on from prohibition of the act towards understanding the impact. The defined terms of reference:

- The factors influencing the increase in suicide rates, with a focus on particularly at-risk groups
- The social and economic costs of suicide and attempted suicide
- The measures necessary to tackle increasing suicide rates, and the barriers to doing so – in particular the Committee will consider the role of:
  1. Local authorities and partner organisations, including police, transport police, the rail industry, fire services, schools, youth services, and drug and alcohol services
  2. Mental health services and other parts of secondary care, including A&E and psychiatric liaison services
  3. Primary care services
  4. Referrals from non-statutory services – local support groups, faith groups, carers, friends and family
  5. Examples of best practice, including those from other countries
- Media reporting of suicide, the effectiveness of guidelines for the reporting of suicide, and the role of social media and suicidal content online
- The value of data collection for suicide prevention, and the action necessary to improve the collection of data on suicide.

While giving evidence to this committee,[14] Mr Hunt[15] proposed a solution to tackling the issue of young people "self-producing" indecent images:

> I just ask myself the simple question as to why it is that you can't prevent the texting of sexually explicit images by people under the age of 18, if that's a lock that parents choose to put on a mobile phone contract. Because there is technology that can identify sexually explicit pictures and prevent it being transmitted … I think there are a lot of things where social media companies could put options in their software that could reduce the risks associated with social media, and I do think that this is something which they should actively pursue in a way that hasn't happened to date.

13 UK House of Commons Health Committee (2017). "Suicide Prevention". https://publica tions.parliament.uk/pa/cm201617/cmselect/cmhealth/1087/1087.pdf
14 Ibid.
15 House of Commons Health Committee (2016). "Oral evidence: Suicide prevention, HC 300". http://data.parliament.uk/writtenevidence/committeeevidence.svc/evidencedoc ument/health-committee/suicide-prevention/oral/44159.html

Returning to the five points detailed at the start of this book, we can clearly see all five in effect here:

1. Policy directions will generally focus upon prohibitive approaches – Mr Hunt is proposing preventing young people from producing "indecent" images on their phones
2. Technology does not solve social problems – Mr Hunt is calling for a technical solution to a social problem, something we will explore in far more detail below
3. In a vacuum of evidence, opinions become an adequate substitute for facts – Mr Hunt is making unsubstantiated claims about the capabilities of technology
4. Everyone has an opinion of how digital technology might best be "made safe" – Mr Hunt is proposing a solution that is not technically possible while stating very clearly that it is
5. Statutory pressure can sometimes result in a "do anything" attitude – a proposal that platform providers should implement a technical "solution" to this issue has an implied suggestion of regulation might be instigated if service providers do not "actively pursue" such "solutions"

However, a more detailed, and evidence-based, exploration of Mr Hunt's statement raises a number of concerns.

First, Mr Hunt proposes that the mobile device should prevent the sending of indecent images. By which means is Mr Hunt referring? Is he just talking about the in-built messaging platforms that form part of the mobile communications platform – such as MMS? Should the interception occur when the image is taken via one of the cameras on the phone to prevent the image being stored in the first place? Or perhaps he is also referring to app-based image exchange on platforms such as WhatsApp, Kik or Snapchat? In which case is he suggesting the underlying technology of the phone should in some way interface with the apps on the phone to determine whether the app-based messaging platform is about to send an indecent image? What about other apps capable of sending an image, such as email? And would the expectation also be to manage image exchange functionality that is accessible through a web browser such as web-based email? And what about other image exchange mechanisms like Bluetooth or Apple's airdrop?

Even at a purely technical level, it is clear to see that there would be a massive effort needed to shut down all possible dissemination routes for an indecent image. It is not simply a case of "preventing it from being transmitted" – transmission can have many forms and these forms are constantly evolving.

Regardless of the fundamental technical challenge, there are another couple of problems that occur when exploring Mr Hunt's "solution" in more detail. First, the idea that all young people have mobile devices that have been registered as being used by a minor. It is certainly the case that mobile devices can be purchased by parents for young people and those phones will be installed with content filters and similar. However, there is also a massive second-hand market for phones, and phones are also passed between family members (for example, when a parent receives an upgrade they will pass their old phone to their child), and certain types of phone ownership will have little indication of the age of the user. While it might be a simple thing to say, "any phone where the user is under the age of 18 should have these countermeasures", the reality is far more problematic. If we are to expect such demands to be placed into legislation, to whom would it fall to ensure that mobile phone records were kept up to date and reflect the age of the user? The parents, the mobile provider, the handset seller?

Moving on to probably the most concerning statement by Mr Hunt – that algorithms exist to identify an indecent image of a minor on the device. While this text is by no means an in-depth exploration of the capabilities of image recognition, we are essentially faced with two different approaches – hashing or statistical/artificial intelligence techniques.[16]

Hashing applies a mathematical process to the data in the file to generate a unique value for that specific image. This algorithm might be applied to, for example, the colour of each pixel in the image, the different colours in the image, keywords associated with the images or image filenames often referred to as "feature extraction". The resulting hash value is an alphanumeric sequence (typically 32 characters in length), that is, due to the application of the algorithm to the data and metadata on an image, hopefully unique, or at least close to unique. It is analogous to a digital fingerprint that identifies the image. Therefore, when the image is found in another location, or shared from a device, hashing carried out on the image data and metadata will result in the same hash. In essence, the technique creates a "fingerprint" for a given image. And if the image is discovered on other platforms, running the algorithm on the image copy will return the same "fingerprint" and the software system can be confident that they are copies of the same image.

While hashing used to rely on an exact copy of the image to produce the same hash value, some, such as Microsoft PhotoDNA,[17] are resistant to slight changes to the image (for example, changes in colour, making the image black and white or changing its size) and one can see the use of such technologies in things like the detection of previously identified child abuse images. Therefore, it could be argued that there is some value in detecting indecent images of minors on mobile devices. However, the detection would rely upon the fact that the image had previously been hashed and stored in a database. Therefore, a self-produced image by a minor, which had never been hashed, would render the technology useless until it is posted somewhere and hashed.

For statistical or artificial intelligence-based techniques, it is generally acknowledged that convolutional neural networks are the best approach for image

---

16 Rui, Yong, Thomas S. Huang, and Shih-Fu Chang (1999). "Image retrieval: Current techniques, promising directions, and open issues". *Journal of Visual Communication and Image Representation*, *10*(1), 39–62.

17 https://www.microsoft.com/en-us/photodna

recognition.[18] As with all artificial intelligence techniques used for image recognition, the algorithm does not recognise images in the same way a human brain might, but instead determines the probability that the data composition in one image, or objects in an image, are similar to other images it has been shown of a type. Usually, this is down to feeding in a large number of sample images for the algorithm to be "trained".[19] The larger and more comprehensive the training set, the more accurate the image recognition when shown new images. Algorithms are not recognising the new image, they are considering how similar the data in the image is to other images. For example, face recognition in applications such as Facebook is successful because the platform already has a collection of images of the subject either posted by themselves or by others who then tag the subject.[20] There, the facial recognition algorithm on the platform has a good level of identifiable images of the subject which it can then match with new images, processing against the generated template of the subject. The more images and tags of the subject, the more accurate the algorithm becomes. While there have been advances in the techniques used for image recognition,[21] the fundamental approach of feeding training sets into an algorithm so it can "learn" about the sorts of images it can recognise still remains. Facial recognition systems that are less subject specific tend to struggle more with false positives. For example, there has been much discussion about the use of facial recognition at public events by the UK police,[22] particularly when used to try to identify criminal suspects, and how inaccurate the systems are (in the case of the news story, 102 individuals were identified as potential suspects yet none were arrested). It is no surprise, given the nature of image recognition systems, that these are not successful – it is highly unlikely the police will have as many images of a suspected individual as, for example, Facebook. Moreover, they are looking at live image recognition in a public setting, so there will be lots of "noise" in the data. Image recognition is simply not sufficiently resilient to be used in these environments.

Furthermore, when considering how an algorithm might be "trained", we can see further concerns about the impact on children's rights. Given, as discussed above, we know that the "best" image recognition algorithms become

18 Stallkamp, J., Schlipsing, M., Salmen, J., and Igel, C. (2012). "Man vs. computer: Benchmarking machine learning algorithms for traffic sign recognition". *Neural networks*, *32*, 323–332.
19 Russakovsky, O., Deng, J., Su, H., Krause, J., Satheesh, S., Ma, S., Huang, Z., Karpathy, A., Khosla, A., Bernstein, M., and Berg, A. C. (2015). "Imagenet large scale visual recognition challenge". *International Journal of Computer Vision*, *115*(3), 211–252.
20 Facebook (2017). "Managing Your Identity on Facebook with Face Recognition Technology". https://newsroom.fb.com/news/2017/12/managing-your-identity-on-facebook-with-face-recognition-technology/
21 Szegedy, C., Ioffe, S., Vanhoucke, V., and Alemi, A.A. (2017). "Inception-v4, inception-resnet and the impact of residual connections on learning". https://arxiv.org/abs/1602.07261v2.
22 Fox, C. (2018). "Face Recognition Police Tools 'staggeringly inaccurate'". *BBC News*. https://www.bbc.com/news/technology-44089161

increasingly successful when they are fed training images that can be statistically and compositionally similar to those it wishes to detect, therefore, if we wish an algorithm to detect indecent images of minors, surely, we would have to train it with similar images? While we might argue that a training set of intimate images of adults might suffice, we have seen that even with the best systems for nudity detection, false positives are unacceptably high. The more accurately the training set is representative of the images it wishes to detect, the greater the accuracy. Therefore, we would assume that the training set must be comprised of indecent images of minors. Images that, at least partially, would have to be illegal. Although given the ambiguity of the legal definition of indecency, discussed below, we might struggle to have a comprehensive set of "indecent" images of children, we might assume that the training set must comprise of, generally, self-generated nude and semi-nude images of minors. Where would a commercial provider gain access to these images? How do the subjects of the images consent to these images being used in training sets (an ethical debate outside of the scope of this book, but a serious one that deserves deep exploration), or are we suggesting that law enforcement agencies provide access to their databases (for example, the Interpol International Child Sexual Exploitation [ICSE] Database[23] has an increasing number of "self-generated" images[24]) for commercial purposes? It is a legal and ethical minefield if we are to consider this approach from an informed perspective.

Returning to Mr Hunt's claim that algorithms exist that can identify indecent images of children and young people, there is a more fundamental issue – the definition for "indecency" in a manner that might be expressed either in an image training set or an algorithm. From a rights and legal perspective, this is extremely problematic. Initially, let us take a human interpretation of this problem – could we, as humans, make consistent, accurate decisions on whether or not a self-generated image is indecent? Could a group of ten individuals all come up with the same categorisation of images that are "decent" and "indecent" if they were presented with a sample? We would suggest that this would be unlikely. Legally speaking, we would struggle for a definitive threshold for "indecency"? While the Coroners and Justice Act 2009 (section 62) sets out to define what a prohibited image of a child is:[25]

1. That the image is pornographic;
2. That the image is grossly offensive, disgusting, or otherwise of an obscene character; and

23 https://www.interpol.int/Crime-areas/Crimes-against-children/Victim-identification
24 ECPAT International (2018). Towards a Global Indicator on Unidentified Victims in Child Sexual Exploitation Material: Technical Report. http://www.ecpat.org/wp-content/upl oads/2018/02/Technical-Report-TOWARDS-A-GLOBAL-INDICATOR-ON-UNIDE NTIFIED-VICTIMS-IN-CHILD-SEXUAL-EXPLOITATION-MATERIAL.pdf
25 UK Government (2009). "Coroners and Justice Act 2009". http://www.legislation.go v.uk/ukpga/2009/25/section/62

3. That the image focuses solely or principally on a child's genitals or anal region, or portrays a number of defined sexual acts, namely:
   * the performance by a person of an act of intercourse or oral sex with or in the presence of a child;
   * an act of masturbation by, of, involving or in the presence of a child;
   * an act which involves penetration of the vagina or anus of a child with a part of a person's body or with anything else;
   * an act of penetration, in the presence of a child, of the vagina or anus of a person with a part of a person's body or with anything else;
   * the performance by a child of an act of intercourse or oral sex with an animal (whether dead or alive or imaginary);
   * the performance by a person of an act of intercourse or oral sex with an animal (whether dead or alive or imaginary) in the presence of a child

This is a subset of what one might consider to be indecent. "Sexting" images might fall into these categories of prohibited images of minors. However, this definition would not work for a large proportion of the sorts of images young people, in our experience, describe as sexting. For example, images of the top half of the body, photographs of the subject in their underwear, sexualised, but not sexually explicit images. Is there, therefore, a need for another definition of what an indecent image is within the sexting context? Should that threshold be set as naked parts of the body? Could a naked image ever not be indecent? Or perhaps underwear? And if that is the case, should swimwear also be included in our threshold? Should we have an arbiter of decency whose judgement is final on these matters, even though there is a risk that perfectly innocent images may be ruled as indecent within our definitions?

While legal definitions are effective for the judicial process when we are determining the legality of an image, if we extend our definition to indecent, are they effective at defining algorithmic constraints to identify an indecent image? Could we define, completely, in a code-based ruleset, what an algorithm should identify as indecent? One cannot have ambiguity or interpretation in an algorithm, algorithms are very bad at addressing these things. Or perhaps we should rely on an elusive, almost certainly, illegal training set to address our problem? Mr Hunt might claim that service providers might have "*technology that can identify sexually explicit pictures and prevent it being transmitted*", the *informed* reality is far more complex.

And perhaps crucially, is there a desire for private sector organisations to scan a minor's phone and make moral judgements based upon an algorithm? Surely one cannot expect politicians to decide that these organisations should make decisions on behalf of a minor based upon a poorly defined rule set and deep inspection of data on the child's mobile device?

That is not to say that all algorithmic approaches to image detection are ineffective and that service providers are doing as much as they can. However, the policy space seems to almost entirely focus on the need of service providers to keep "doing more". Using technology where it has strength, such as pattern matching and data comparison, is undoubtedly a positive intervention and one that could go further. Given that PhotoDNA can generate a unique hash value for images run against the algorithm, once an image has been hashed, there is no reason why the service provider could not identify the image if it was reposted.

If one is to consider protection for victims of revenge pornography where a disgruntled partner repeatedly shares an image on a social media site, the technology is there to hash the image when first posted and scan for similar hashes on reposted images. In such cases, it seems perfectly reasonable to expect the service provider to be able to detect reposts and facilitate removal without the need for the victim to rediscover the image and potentially experience revictimisation.

Share Your Images with Us to Prevent Others From Seeing Them

When considering the broader issue of revenge pornography, there remains pressure on social media companies to "do more" to protect victims of harm that arises from the non-consensual sharing of intimate images in a more proactive manner. There have been calls[26] to ensure that this media is not posted in the first place or to automate the takedown process so that victims do not have to experience repeated discoveries of the shared images and make numerous takedown reports. There is certainly evidence, from the Revenge Porn Helpline,[27] that social media companies are far more responsive to takedown requests than they have been historically. However, there is still a requirement for a report to take down the image before an investigation is mounted and only then, in the event that "community standards" have been breached, will the media be removed.

Nevertheless, even with approaches which make sense from a technical perspective, there is sometimes evidence of these technologies being used in curious ways, arguably as a result of political pressure and the need for organisations to show they are "doing more".

At the start of November 2017, Facebook, along with the Australian eSafety Commission, announced a pilot project that would add another level of proactivity to addressing revenge pornography concerns.[28] The proposed pilot system, initially solely in Australia, provides the facilities for users to share their self-generated intimate images with Facebook and use hashing techniques to ensure that further reposting is not possible. The basic steps of the proposed system are:

26 Daily Mail (2017). "Facebook 'must not be a haven for paedophiles': Home Secretary's warning over vile images on Social Network". *The Daily Mail*. http://www.dailymail.co.u k/news/article-4410462/Facebook-not-haven-paedophiles.html
27 https://revengepornhelpline.org.uk
28 Davis, A. (2017). "The Facts: Non-Consensual Intimate Image Pilot". https://newsroo m.fb.com/news/h/non-consensual-intimate-image-pilot-the-facts/

- Australians can complete an online form on the eSafety Commissioner's official website.
- To establish which image is of concern, people will be asked to send the image to themselves on Messenger.
- The eSafety Commissioner's office notifies us of the submission (via their form). However, they do not have access to the actual image.
- Once we receive this notification, a specially trained representative from our Community Operations team reviews and hashes the image, which creates a human-unreadable, numerical fingerprint of it.

Facebook stressed that the image is not retained for any longer than it takes to evaluate and hash the image, the only thing that is stored long term is the hash itself. As a final step in the process, once the hash is complete and stored, the sender of the image is informed so they can remove the image from Messenger, and at that point, Facebook will remove the image from their database.

Therefore, if there is a case of someone else trying to share that image on Facebook when the image is hashed and compared against the user uploaded intimate image hashes, and there is a match, the image will not be posted and the intended poster will be informed their upload infringes community standards. In that way, the approach "protects" the person in the image from exposure by others.

While this is an interesting concept, and does show how existing proven technology can be used to provide an element of protection for those wishing to protect themselves from the risk of exposure, it does also demonstrate how, if left to service providers, their only route to protection is technological (unless such a platform employs human intervention prior to *anything* being uploaded, which is possibly exorbitantly resource intensive).

One can reflect upon a few potential issues with this approach, by way of illustration of this point. We have discussed at length the difference between adult non-consensual sharing and teen "sexting", particularly the challenges in legislation and how this presents more challenges to protect the victim as a result. Furthermore, there is a high likelihood that images shared by young people among their peers may end up being posted on social media. Therefore, one can realistically assume that young people might view the proposed approach by Facebook as one that could be used to ensure they are protected from the risk of spreading images of themselves. Of course, this poses a serious problem to the "solution" provider – if young people are sharing self-generated images with Facebook, the provider is, in essence, facilitating the distribution of indecent images of minors. The subsequent storing of these images further breaks child protection laws – the duration of storage is not something defined in the covering statutes, it is any storage of indecent images of minors that defines the criminality.

While the provider might argue that, given there is a vetting process which will check the profile of the user who is uploading the images, they verify age via the profile, much has been written about the struggle all social media providers face with age verification on their systems. There are many "under-aged" users on these social media platforms, and the means by which most social media providers verify age (asking at sign up for a date of birth) is hardly rigorous. And while a provider might argue that any user lying about their age on sign up is invalidating the terms and conditions of use, and therefore, their right to protection, it would be a very brave defence in the event of providing a "solution" to revenge pornography that potentially encourages the distribution and storage, however transient, of indecent images of minors.

Further complexity and concern are compounded with the move into the perennial legal and moral debate around who determines the indecency of the image and makes the judgement on whether it should be hashed and stored. While Facebook has stated that "*a specially trained representative from our Community Operations team reviews and hashes the image*", the review process itself is not defined, nor are the thresholds for indecency. What would be the situation where a user flagged an image for hashing they believed was placing them at risk, but the reviewer decided that the image was not intimate "enough" to be hashed. Who makes the decision on decency? The image owner or the platform provider? There are cultural differences around indecency – for example, a Western perspective on indecency might be different from one from an Asian one. While nudity might be a threshold for some, cleavage might be sufficient in another. And while legal indecency may not be met, the impact on the victim in the event of the sharing of such images may still be equally severe.

Following on from this, the owner of the image also raises some concerns – for example, if one is to state that the image has to be self-generated in order for Facebook to be able to hash the image and store it, can we assume that intimate images of individuals taken, for example, by a partner are not covered? What would happen then if a vexatious ex-partner, with a collection of images they had taken of the victim, decides to share those images on the platform? An assumption must be made that this protection mechanism would not be open to the victim in this scenario, because the copyright for the image lies with the taker of the image, not the subject in the image (as defined in the Copyright, Designs and Patents Act 1988[29]) as long as the subject consented, at the time, to the image being taken. In essence, this protection will only work for "selfies". Once potential abusers are aware of this, their approach to abuse will simply switch to sharing images for which they retain copyright.

Even in this brief review of the issues, from a legislative and technical perspective, we can see that the solution is not without significant problems. And while efforts by service providers to think about how technology can be used to help victims should be applauded, pure technological solutions are always going to struggle within complex social systems. In essence, the pressure on service providers to "do more" is resulting in surrogates implemented in code rather than addressing the issues with a multi-stakeholder approach drawn from effective

---

29 UK Government (1998). "Copyright, Designs and Patents Act 1998". http://www.legislati on.gov.uk/ukpga/1988/48/contents

social policy. However, the more fundamental issue around this "solution" that lies at the heart of victim blaming within sexting and revenge pornography scenarios is responsibility.

As already discussed, what is clear with a lot of revenge pornography victims is that they will blame themselves for the redistribution of the image. Many victims will state that by taking the image they placed themselves at risk, and it was, therefore, their fault their abuser had the image to share or use for further harassment. As reported in Chapter 2, across the UK, Australia and New Zealand, 70% of young people surveyed (n=700) say the responsibility of the image lies with the maker (and usually subject) of the image.

By communicating to the population that the way to protect yourself from the dangers of abuse from revenge pornography is to share the image with a third party, who will put in measures to ensure if someone does share the image, they might be able to stop it, surely one is saying the responsibility for the control and management of the image lies with the victim? There are two messages given out by this:

> We have provided you with a means to protect yourself from someone else sharing images you might have taken of yourself on our platform. if you don't engage with this solution, it will be your fault if someone posts it on our platform.

And perhaps more confusingly:

> If you want to protect yourself from someone sharing images of you, you need to first share the image with someone else. But don't worry, we can be trusted. But don't share with anyone else, because they can't be, unless you share with us first!

These messages are surely just further ways of showing the victim that responsibility for the non-consensual sharing of an image lies with them unless they do something further to protect themselves. This harks back to the sort of messages young people talk about when they raise the non-consensual sharing of images with adults supposedly responsible for their safeguarding – "well, you shouldn't have done that should you!?"

When it comes to legalities, there are clear and socially acceptable boundaries. If one considers copyright infringements, there is a clear process. Owners must identify where their material exists online in breach of copyright, and human intervention must determine the owner's rights to a takedown – this is an approach that exists on mainstream platforms such as YouTube and also, as already discussed, on pornography platforms – it is how they provide takedown routes around revenge pornography. If the content poster objects, this can be challenged in law. But in all cases, there is clear accountability – the owner is responsible for asserting a breach, the author is responsible for defending the right to publish and both must accept a court's ruling. While the process might be cumbersome, it ensures rights are protected and infringements can be debated.

With child abuse material in online spaces, there is a similar expectation via organisations such as the Internet Watch Foundation (IWF), who will respond to reports and make decisions on legality. The IWF make these judgements based upon reports from the public and are carried out by humans. The organisation now also has proactive powers to search for content and add to its watch lists without reporting.

Yet the policy direction now seems to be moving away from this to expect almost a complete bypassing of human intervention, and certainly the involvement of the courts, to insist service providers make judgements on content in communications or posted on their platforms and automate takedowns based on algorithmic interpretation. This is doomed to fail. Ultimately, these platforms are providing spaces where abuse, bullying and harassment can occur as a result of, for example, the communication of a self-generated intimate image. However, these behaviours can only be judged effectively within a legislative framework implemented in law enforcement. Law enforcement can make judgements on the severity of abuse, move to prosecute and make interventions to mitigate future bad behaviour. One cannot expect private sector organisations to make these judgements and be responsible for intervention and control, bypassing the legislative process, as they do not have the capacity to do so without seriously impacting upon the quality of the end-user experience and users' rights.

Surely the focus of control, and technical intervention, should lie with ensuring that others cannot non-consensually share intimate images of others and, if they do, there will be consequences for doing so. This should be implemented in line with more effective public communication, legislation and stronger sentencing of those who choose to share images of others without consent. We fear that this "solution" just places more pressure on the victim to ensure they protect themselves and the responsibility for protection lies with them.

What Is Actually Possible?

While there are many excessive expectations on service providers by those who perhaps do not grasp the social and technical complexity of what is being asked, there are things that platform providers can do with technology that does not, yet, happen by default.

One such potential step forward in protecting those who become victims of non-consensual sharing was illustrated in a recently out of court settlement between a teenage girl in Belfast and Facebook.[30] The case was formed from a complaint from the girl, who was 14 at the time, that she had reported an intimate self-generated image shared a number of times on Facebook by an abuser. Each time the image was reported, Facebook had taken down the image, but the

30 BBC (2018). "Facebook Pays Costs in Naked Photo Settlement". *BBC News.* https://ww w.bbc.co.uk/news/uk-northern-ireland-42627373

abuser would then reshare it.[31] The girl's legal team argued that Facebook had a responsibility to prevent the reposting of images already taken down and that the technology to do this is far less complex than mythical "indecency detection" algorithms – they could simply hash (as discussed earlier in this chapter) the images and if they were reported, a search of the "takedown" hashes would show it had already been reported, judged to have breached standards and should be automatically taken down. This is something that would be straightforward for an algorithm to do because the judgement around the validity of the image would have already been performed.

Why, argued the legal team, could the service provider not hash any image that has been taken down so if someone tries to repost it, the system will detect this and prevent posting? While Facebook argued that they had behaved responsibly in that they had always taken down the images when reported, a case against the company was allowed and the girl sued for misuse of private information, negligence and breach of the Data Protection Act. In early January 2018, the case was settled out of court with Facebook paying all of the girl's legal costs as part of an undisclosed settlement. During the case, Facebook announced a project in the US that will do what has been called for in the case of extremist content, but not intimate, non-consensually shared photographs.[32]

Technology can clearly "do smart things" when applied with a precise logic and clear ruleset. However, claiming that unreliable algorithms are the solution to a problem that can have a significant impact on a child's mental health is, at best, naïve, and, at worst, irresponsible. If pressure and threats of legislation are placed upon service providers, they will certainly respond with "solutions". However, by saying service providers can "do smart things" does not mean that they are capable of providing a technical solution to any policy demand.

Ultimately, the policy perspective, and therefore, the legislative programme, is one of prohibition. The view is predominantly "if we can stop this happening, the individual will be safe". By preventing a situation, by taking down content, by encouraging social media providers to aggressively monitor and censor posts on their sites, do we achieve the goal of a safe online environment? We see proposals for content control, monitoring, age verification, behavioural management and limitations on screen time all as a result of intervention by the technology provider who is implementing such measures under the threat of further legislation if they do not. We are seeing little to propose upskilling the population, addressing the need for effective and broad relationships and sex education in schools, and

31 Belfast Live (2016). Picture of naked 14-year-old from NI was repeatedly posted on Facebook "shame" page, court hears. *Belfast Live*. http://www.belfastlive.co.uk/news/belfast-news/picture-naked-14-year-old-11861938

32 Facebook (2016). "Partnering to Help Curb Spread of Online Terrorist Content". https://newsroom.fb.com/news/2016/12/partnering-to-help-curb-spread-of-online-terrorist-content/

making individual responsibility something that a user might be held accountable for in their online behaviour.

There is a need to take a step back from this ideological obsession with accountability by industry. While industry needs to play its part, and has to have some level of accountability, equally, that cannot provide the solutions. Algorithms cannot make moral judgements, as algorithms deal with absolutes while morality does not. To expect algorithms to make these judgements reflects a failure in understanding how the technology works. Equally, if pressure is placed on service providers to "do something", that something will always be based around technology because that is all they can do.

There is a need to acknowledge the challenges facing the education system in promoting what is healthy and normal in relationships. Our discussions with many children show that relationships and sex education (RSE) has been sadly lacking for many years. While there has been a statutory requirement to teach the biology of reproduction, until recently, anything else taught was at the discretion of the school. With effective RSE, it is unsurprising that young people are engaging in behaviours that we as adults might find bewildering in which young people are engaging. While society might find it outrageous that a boy aged 11 might send a photograph of his genitals to his girlfriend, it should equally acknowledge that perhaps this is because no-one has told him this is not usual practice in a relationship. In Chapter 7, this complex issue is explored in more detail.

7 What About Education?

Chapter 6 explored the role of the service/platform providers in protecting their users from harm that resulted from the non-consensual sharing of images, drawing the focus of responsibility from political discourse that demands that these providers must "do more". It also highlighted that such demands place unrealistic expectations on these providers who can, at best, provide technological intervention, reporting routes and takedown processes. They cannot prevent an image from being taken, sent, shared or used to abuse, regardless of what some politicians might claim "clever algorithms" can do.

The policy perspective has failed to effectively consider the fact that what young people tell us is most important – effective education delivered by knowledgeable and responsive professionals. Throughout this book there has been an exploration of the perspectives on education from a number of stakeholders, including politicians, safeguarding professionals, police and educators. Almost unanimously, we can see calls for more effective education. Whether dealing with youth or adult victims of image-based abuse, many make it clear they have no knowledge of the law, their rights, the acceptability of what have become somewhat normalised social behaviours or even recognition of the fact that what they are doing might be abusive, let alone illegal. The impact of an educative approach that utilises a punitive focus has also been explored – adult victims of image-based abuse use the rhetorical from their educational experiences to blame themselves in the event someone has non-consensually shared intimate images of them.

Is "Self-Generation" Part of the Problem?

Perhaps one of the fundamental issues faced is the fact that even the terminology lays blame with the victim. The use of the term revenge pornography has already been discussed at length, and how the use of *revenge* implies that in some way there is justification for the abuser – that they are getting revenge for harm to them caused by the victim. We would further extend this criticism of terminology to the words used in the public conscience around the act of producing the image in the first place – "self-generated" or, in the case of teen sexting, "youth produced".

As previously discussed, youth "sexting" behaviours have become an established facet of child and adolescent experiences, and are often associated with harmful outcomes – discussions with young people highlight that "sexting incidents" are regular, widely known and highly visible to pupils in school settings.[1] By the same token, law enforcement experiences of the investigations of sexual images of children speak to the reality that so-called "self-generated" or "youth-produced" images and videos have become a common aspect within the wider child sexual abuse and exploitation material in circulation.[2]

The response of both policymakers and educators is often to emphasise the prohibition of the "sexting" practice and turns around the assumption that these behaviours are inherently harmful. As already discussed, educational approaches and media messages tend to focus on the illegality of the "sexting" practice and emphasise the notion that young people are essentially breaking the law if they "self-generate" or produce a sexual image of themselves. These messages rarely achieve the intended impact – young people say they do little to prevent those wishing to produce and share images from doing so. More importantly, such messaging becomes counterproductive when victims of abuse and exploitation arising from the dissemination of their imagery are harmed, yet do not wish to disclose their experiences to those who might help them. Throughout this book, there have been descriptions of the feelings of victims of both teen sexting and revenge pornography and they will, on many occasions, blame themselves for the non-consensual redistribution of these images. Survey work already discussed (from both 2009[3] and 2017[4]) has consistently shown that most young people believe responsibility for the image lies with the taker, not the sharer – a fairly consistent 70% of young people surveyed have this belief. Moreover, the Revenge Porn Helpline frequently reports victims saying if they had not taken the images (or given into the demands and pressure from their would-be abuser), then the abuser would not be in a position to share the image further.

While image generation *might* be entirely self-motivated and voluntary, it might also arise as a result of external pressure, coercion, exploitation or extortion. In some cases, while the subject of the image might have produced it, the motivation for this production might be a result of, for example, coercion from an abuser with some form of control over the victim. For example, 19-year-old Zeeshan Aqsar[5] used an indecent image he had pressured his 15-year-old victim

1 Phippen, A. (2012). "Sexting: An Exploration of Practices, Attitudes and influences". *NSPCC.* https://www.nspcc.org.uk/globalassets/documents/research-reports/sexting-exploration-practices-attitudes-influences-report-2012.pdf
2 US Sentencing Commission (2012). "Testimony of Michelle Collins". https://www.ussc.gov/sites/default/files/pdf/amendment-process/public-hearings-and-meetings/20120215-16/Testimony_15_Collins.pdf
3 Ibid.
4 Ibid.
5 Daily Mail (2015). "Law student, 19, convinced teenage girl to send him an X-rated picture then used it to blackmail her for more photos and money". *The Daily Mail.* http://www.dail

into sharing with him to try to extort further images and money from her. Harry Sloan[6] adopted a similar approach, while further compounding the exploitation of his victims by posing as a teenage girl to deceive and coerce young boys into producing and sending indecent images to him, as well as money.

In more recent survey work, over 65% of youth respondents reported that "pressure" was one of the main reasons that young people send "nudes".[7] One might also reflect on social pressures as a means to induce a "self-generated" image – in the same survey work, one of the most popular responses to the question "Why do you think people send nudes" was "To get a boyfriend/girlfriend". While this is not a coercive factor in the traditional sense, it should be acknowledged that the formation of relationships, and the associated desire to feel attractive, is a social pressure to send these sorts of images.

Furthermore, the UK Government's own sexting response guidance for schools produced by UKCCIS[8] describes "youth produced sexual images" as best practice terminology:

"Youth produced sexual imagery" best describes the practice because:

- "Youth produced" includes young people sharing images that they, or another young person, have created of themselves.
- "Sexual" is clearer than "indecent". A judgement of whether something is 'decent' is both a value judgement and dependent on context.
- "Imagery" covers both still photos and moving videos (and this is what is meant by reference to imagery throughout the document).

With no caveat around production perhaps being involuntary or coerced.

Clearly, the focus of blame, and any subsequent punishment, should reside with those who abuse or exploit sexual imagery, not those who are victimised in these cases. Yet this does not always seem to be the case in non-consensual sharing scenarios. "Self-produced" implies free will. And that is not necessarily the case.

---

ymail.co.uk/news/article-3277297/Law-student-19-convinced-teenage-girl-send-X-rated-picture-used-blackmail-photos-money.html

6 Madden, S. (2017). "Jailed: Four years for 'dangerous' teenager who posed as a girl then threatened boys over indecent images". *Shropshire Star*. https://www.shropshirestar.com/news/crime/2017/09/20/jailed-four-years-for-dangerous-teenager-who-posed-as-a-girl-then-threatened-boys-over-indecent-images/

7 Ibid.

8 UKCCIS (2017). "Sexting in schools and colleges: Responding to incidents and safeguarding young people". https://assets.publishing.service.gov.uk/government/uploads/system/uploads/attachment_data/file/609874/6_2939_SP_NCA_Sexting_In_Schools_FINAL_Update_Jan17.pdf

Are Educational Approaches Working?

Within the UK, the education system is currently failing young people in their calls for up to date, effective and responsible relationships and sex education which incorporates issues such as sexting. When embarking on early research in sexting,[9] there was a prevalent theme of victim blaming, and the lack of appreciation around what the impact of their intimate images being widely shared might be. Many of the viewed images were not shared further to abuse or harm. When asked what adults could do to help the prevalent response was "listen, understand and don't judge".

In further research in 2012,[10] the comments were similar, as was the victim blaming, and awareness that sending nudes was illegal. When asked what adults could do to help victims of abuse, the prevailing view was once again the need for adults to "listen, understand and don't judge".

These responses were replicated in further work in 2017.[11] Both statistics and prevailing victim blaming views were the same. As were the views around how adults might best support young people. In approximately ten years, young people have been giving a very clear message to those tasked with their safeguarding, and they have not been receiving it. With this evidence, it can be shown how educational approaches have not changed in this time, and young people do not believe they are working.

In these discussions with young people and education professionals about how to tackle harms arising from the non-consensual sharing of images, it is rare that they call for technological intervention or more online tools. In one discussion group with a group of sixth form children when the discussion around both behaviours and legislation related to image-based abuse, one 16-year-old male observed that the only time they get to discuss anything to do with sex and relationships is when an external provider visits the school for a "specialist" delivery. The young man observed that there are no teachers at the school who deliver any education around sex and relationships. This was an attitude reflected in many other school settings – they are either told sending nudes is illegal or an external provider will visit the school, answer a few questions, then leave.

In general, as already discussed earlier in this text, schools play lip service to the non-consensual sharing of intimate images and image-based abuse, generally with an assembly or a visit from an external speaker (invariably a member of law enforcement), who will reinforce messages around the legalities of the taking and sharing of images, and perhaps some basic prohibitive messages. And there also seems to be a gulf between "online safety" messages and those related to relationships education – young people disclose "terrifying" talks by police about

9 Ibid.
10 Ibid.
11 Ibid.

how sending nudes can end in suicide, tedious assemblies where they are shown a video that is supposed to make them realise sending nudes is wrong and the only aspect of sex and relationships they discuss centres on reproduction and contraception.

However, issues such as victim blaming were rarely discussed, and there was a dearth of knowledge of rights to protection or anything other than the standard "do not do it it's illegal" mantra that is passed off as education around the legalities of sending nudes, which lead to attitudes of fault on the part of the sender and, as we hear equally from victims of revenge pornography, it's their fault for taking the image in the first place.

There are many calls from young people to provide effective education around teen sexting, but also that the law is failing them and making them too scared to disclose abuse because they have been told if they self-produce an image they will end up on the sex offender register. What "effective" education would look like is something we have discussed with young people a great deal. For example, what sort of age should this start from, what do they think should be covered and how should it be delivered?

They are generally very clear that these sorts of issues need to be discussed at primary school, albeit in an age-appropriate way. They also feel that such education needs to be delivered by staff who know what they are talking about and are specialists in this area. One area of positive learning, at many schools we visit, occurs when schools engage with the services of a relationships education expert. As already mentioned, a lot of schools will use the services of external agencies who deliver sex and relationship education on specialist days. In other instances, young people have talked about independent specialists who are commissioned by schools.

The format generally used in these sessions is "bite-sized" interactive sessions that cover many different aspects of relationships education, such as healthy relationships, STIs, contraception and different gender relationships. However, the key messages all hinge on issues such as consent (verbal and non-verbal), trust and the importance of saying no in relationships. Within these sessions, online issues are raised (such as the difference between consensually and non-consensually sharing an image or pornography), but the focus is on what is positive and healthy in relationships, and what is harmful, "poor" or even abusive. A lot of young people talk about the importance of being able to ask questions in these sessions and, perhaps more importantly, to have them answered.

The general view of these specialist days is that they are, on the whole, very positive experiences because the people who are delivering the education know what they are talking about and do not shy away from difficult or potentially embarrassing questions. However, equally, there is no standard or legislative requirement for anyone visiting a school to deliver this education to be qualified to do so, aside from the standard safeguarding expectations of a criminal record check.

When further exploring with young people what a "sexting" lesson would look like, they frequently talk about the need for greater understanding around the behaviours associated with the act, rather than simply focusing on the act and the associated fall out or the legalities of the act. Issues such as self-esteem, peer pressure, respect and boundaries and, perhaps most importantly, consent. As discussed earlier in the text, the concept that consent can be passed on, or is *transferable* alongside an image, is something that is both commonly perceived and problematic. Many young people (and also given statements from victims from the Revenge Porn Helpline, adults) believe that consent is passed on with the image, such that the receiver has received consent to share further. However, if this is discussed with them, it soon becomes clear to them that this is a ridiculous concept. In the same way that sexual consent exists only in a single situation (i.e. one cannot argue because they have had sex with someone once, they are entitled to have sex again whenever they like), the receipt of an image with the consent of the sender/producer does not mean the recipient now has carte blanche to do whatever they like with the image.

Young people tell us that their educational experiences around sexting are poor, but moreover, their experiences about relationships in general are. They tell us that there are no "safe spaces" to explore issues around sexting, to ask questions and have them answered around the law – they are simply told the repeated educational mantra:

You shouldn't do it, it's illegal.

While there are resources available that challenge that perception, for example, So You Got Naked Online[12] by SWGfL, these are often disregarded in favour of a simpler message of illegality. There seems little surprise that this is the case – without legislative support, such as was provided regarding a teacher's search and confiscation powers in s2 Education Act 2011,[13] any message other than "don't send nudes, it's illegal" potentially places the teacher in a professionally vulnerable position. By the letter of the law, teen sexting is illegal, this needs to be said. If a member of staff, without professional and legislative protection, was to conduct a class that began "While it is illegal, it is not usually the case that a young person will be prosecuted for engaging in these practices", one might anticipate the response of parents and potentially the media. Similar media storms have happened in the past, such as one around a teacher highlighting privacy issues among pupils by showing what images he collected of them from public posts.[14] The professional risk for teachers, particularly around sensitive subjects, is very

---

12 SWGfL (2019). "So You Got Naked Online". https://swgfl.org.uk/resources/so-you-go t-naked-online/

13 UK Government (2011). "s2. Education Act 2011". http://www.legislation.gov.uk/ukpga /2011/21/section/2/enacted

14 Robinson (2014). "Schoolgirl, 15, humiliated by teacher who showed a picture of her in a bikini to 100 fellow pupils to demonstrate dangers social networks". *The Daily Mail.* https ://www.dailymail.co.uk/news/article-2782126/Schoolgirl-15-humiliated-teacher-sho wed-picture-bikini-100-fellow-pupils-demonstrate-dangers-social-networks.html

real and can have significant impacts on careers. Therefore, it is no wonder they err on the side of caution.

However, as already discussed, the "don't send nudes, it's illegal" message is inaccurate because it does not provide the full picture (public interest, outcome 21, etc.). Moreover, it is harmful to victims. If a young person is being abused as a result of an image they shared, they need help. If their school has told them that what they did was illegal, they will not go for help. There is then a risk of further abuse or harm as a result of a poor approach to education that is not, of itself, telling the whole picture of the legal side of sexting among teens.

By having this simple message in schools, the educational approach fails to look at the wider issues around teen sexting, which we see from evidence presented from both youth and also adult, would effectively place the act in a more representative and accurate content. The production and sharing of an image happen for a reason, the re-sharing, non-consensually, equally does. Yet it is extremely rare that young people in a school have had the opportunity to discuss why sexting happens and the negative scenarios that might emerge as a result. Many young people fail to appreciate the exploitative or coercive nature of sending someone a message such as "I've got an image of you, unless you send me more I will share this one" – this is simply viewed as part of online relationships. And while the legislation, particularly in England and Wales, still fails to address the severity of the threat, it can still be evidence of coercion or domestic abuse. While one might argue that surely young people should be aware of this, it "goes without saying", with a dearth of education around relationships, we might equally be guilty or projecting an adult perspective onto young people who have no place to get answers. One young person maturely observed that their sex and relationship lessons helped them understand how not to get pregnant, but they had less appreciation of what healthy behaviour is like in a relationship.

By way of continuity, research with education professionals shows similar views. Drawing upon data collected during research carried out for the Marie Collins Foundation's research into online peer on peer abuse,[15] a number of education professional's responses also raise the need for education to address concerns that technology is facilitating abuse among peers in schools. The responses suggest a staff base who know they have to do "something" but without any guidance, training or national coordination, they're not sure what that "something" might look like. One professional expressed the need for guidance on the differentiation between sexual experimentation and an intention to abuse, which relates to any often-asked question among professionals – "what is normal?"

They, on the one hand, know that they need to support young people growing up in an environment where online abuse is far more likely than when they were young themselves, but equally fear overreaction to issues that "might" be

15 Phippen, A., Bond, E., and Tyrell, K. (2018). "Online Peer on Peer Abuse". *The Marie Collins Foundation.* https://www.mariecollinsfoundation.org.uk/assets/news_entry_featu red_image/MCF-Peer-on-peer-abuse-Research-Report-sunday-final-version.pdf

normal among this generation of youth. The "normalisation" of intimate images distributed by mobile devices is something that attracts discourse among both journalists and scholars (for example,[16],[17]), yet one might argue this is purely derived from the belief that because the behaviour is facilitated by a mobile device, it must be "new". However, the underlying principles of consent, respect, understanding boundaries and respecting the privacy of others are all things that can be understood, and communicated, regardless of the technology emerging for a generation.

These issues are sometimes faced by those who are not expecting to see them and are ill-equipped to deal with them. One respondent to the survey described a difficult safeguarding issue of an 11-year-old child in their care who took and sent an indecent image to a peer, who then shared it with the rest of the class. The respondent said they only discovered this during an informal conversation with a young person in class, and their immediate concern was how to disclose it, as they were very aware they had received no training on such matters and there was no incident response mechanism in the setting.

The issue of the sharing of images within primary settings is one that is occurring more frequently. While it has been commonplace for secondary schools to deal with sexting incidents for over ten years – it is now fairly usual for staff in these settings to encounter image exchange and the fallout therein, and they usually have policy and incident responses in place to deal with it (albeit with little national coordination of decent levels of legal advice). However, encountering image exchanges in primary settings (and sometimes with subsequent sharing) is increasing and these schools tend not to be equipped to deal with them or even have sufficient awareness that this is something that could happen with children in their care. However, as already discussed in Chapter 1, while education professionals might hope that such behaviour wouldn't manifest in their schools, given there is virtually no relationship education currently in the primary setting in the UK, perhaps it is little wonder children might view this as a "normal" part of having a boyfriend or girlfriend or, upon receipt of their first mobile device, think that this is an amusing or even expected thing to do – particularly if they have older siblings or even parents who engage in such practices. Staff can still be ill-equipped to deal with these incidents or even be aware that they might be happening.

Others who responded to the survey acknowledged the need for public education in this area, as they were only a single stakeholder in the safeguarding of young people. They were of the view a public awareness campaign was needed to raise the population's overall knowledge about the sending of nudes, the legal

16 Levine, D. (2013). "Sexting: A terrifying health risk… or the new normal for young adults?". *The Journal of Adolescent Health: Official Publication of the Society for Adolescent Medicine, 52*(3), 257.
17 Döring, N. (2014). "Consensual sexting among adolescents: Risk prevention through abstinence education or safer sexting?". *Cyberpsychology: Journal of Psychosocial Research on Cyberspace, 8*(1). doi: 10.5817/CP2014-1-9

aspects and how to best support young people, and they drew an analogy with the recent campaigns around single-use plastics in the ocean.

This is a valid point – we have seen "public health" issues such as AIDS dealt with through both government awareness campaigns and also weaving public education messages into popular TV shows of the time, which had a great deal of impact. And there has certainly been a sudden and clear shift in public attitudes to single-use plastics as a result of awareness campaigns. However, one might argue that issues around the non-consensual sharing of intimate images, and associated image-based abuse, is less binary that dealing with plastics in the sea. For plastics, it is clear how this can be aligned to Lessig's work[18] around the regulation of social behaviours and the four modalities of law, social norms, market pressures and architecture:

- Laws – simple environmental legislation can be passed to outlaw the disposal of single-use plastics, should the political and social will be sufficient.
- Social norms – it is easy to win over the public with this argument because most citizens care about the environment and can clearly see the impact of non-degrading plastics on the seas (especially when the media is showing images of such).
- Market pressures – as a result of public opinion swaying onto opposition for the disposal of single-use plastics, companies will respond and use social advertising to promote their reduction in plastics use as good public relations and a potential competitive advantage.
- Architecture – the physical space can be managed to encourage recycling and not treat single-use plastics as waste.

However, if we try to apply the same modalities to image-based abuse, we see that this is far more problematic:

- Laws – much of this book has explored why this is an area that is so difficult to legislate – first, we see the tension between the need to protect children and how the literal application of the law punishes them (Protection of Children Act 1978), and even new legislation developed specifically to address the issue of image-based abuse is flawed, due to the need of proof of harm or gratification, and the lack of threat in the England and Wales legislation (Criminal Justice and Courts Act 2015).
- Social norms – there is widely varied public opinion on image-based abuse – some believe that offenders should be punished more harshly, whereas others will blame the victim. There is certainly little uniform public opinion on these behaviours.
- Market pressures – the only place market pressure might be applied is through the service and platform providers, yet service providers can only

---

18 Lessig, L. (1999). "The law of the horse: What cyber law might teach". *Harvard Law Review, 113*, 501.

do so much with technology to prevent these actions, and what little market pressure there is tends to come from victims groups, rather than the public at large – it is unlikely someone will switch networks or platforms because a provider has a poor policy around image-based abuse – it is fairly invisible to the wider public until it either happens to them or someone they know.

- Architecture – there is no physical space, and the virtual space can provide little architectural intervention to manage the problem. One might argue that the architecture around image-based abuse, particularly for young people, might include the stakeholders in their safeguarding. This is an issue that education professionals might come across but are poorly equipped to tackle.

Therefore, while sometimes offline comparisons are useful, in the case of image-based abuse it is flawed. However, the point the staff member was making is a valid one. While there was a public education campaign when the Criminal Justice and Courts Act came to royal ascent,[19] it had little impact and was certainly not something that we have come across in our research with members of the public who work in a safeguarding capacity or with law enforcement. The issues around image-based abuse cannot form a simple message, which is generally what is needed for public awareness campaigns. In essence, the message for adults is:

If you engage in the exchange of indecent images in relationships, there is now a law to protect you should those images be shared further non-consensually.

And for young people:

Young people might exchange indecent images as part of a relationship, as adults do, and sometimes those images are shared non-consensually. While the legislation states that any young person taking an indecent image of themselves and sending it to someone is breaking the law, that law reached ascent in 1978 and was intended to protect, not prosecute minors, so, while illegal, we would rather support a victim of non-consensual sharing than criminalise them.

The message for adults is sufficiently complex, the message regarding teen sexting is certainly not something one might see on a poster at the side of a bus stop.

Nevertheless, the message coming from several staff members who conducted the survey was that this was "just another" thing that teachers were expected to deal with when they have neither the resources nor the training to do so. While they acknowledge that peer on peer abuse as a result of non-consensual sharing

19 UK Government (2015). "The Be Aware B4 You Share campaign". https://assets.publi shing.service.gov.uk/government/uploads/system/uploads/attachment_data/file/4052 86/revenge-porn-factsheet.pdf

was "a tidal wave", with a lack of support and resources, sometimes it was better to "turn a blind eye" than tackling the complexities of the safeguarding situation. One respondent simply stated that they were paid to teach, not police things that happen outside the school gates.

Furthermore, the staff in these settings who are most likely to encounter a disclosure are those least likely to be involved in any training or discussions about whole-school practice. It was, many respondents observed, people in the lower ranks of the staff hierarchy who provide the most day-to-day pastoral support, such as teaching assistants and lunchtime monitors. However, it was equally observed that those individuals are the least likely to receive any safeguarding training or be involved in policy developments.

From two different perspectives – the young people themselves and the staff who are responsible for their safeguarding – there is a frustration about the quality of education and the training of staff. Is it any wonder, with a dearth of knowledge from staff, that they fall back on resources that young people find patronising and boring? While they have a breadth of questions and concerns around image-based abuse, they are still met with standard messages delivered by staff who would rather not be doing so.

The Role of Legislation In Improving Education Provision

Within the UK, there has been much debate around "online safety" education over recent years, and the place for things like the non-consensual sharing of intimate images in this context. As already discussed, young people are crying out for better education in this area. Yet, until recently, there has been little to suggest any further support for education, to develop curriculum further and certainly no mention of the need for specialist teachers in this area.

While the legislative process is improving, and there is greater protection for victims as the criminal justice process adapts to this emerging phenomenon with a greater level of understanding and pragmatism, it will never be a solution, just as the legality of substance abuse does not prevent engagement with such practices.

In exploring UK policy around personal social and health education (PSHE) and sex and relationships education (SRE), there has been little activity until very recently. However, the Education Select Committee did carry out a consultation during 2014 around this provision in schools.[20] The committee announced this inquiry in April 2104, with the following points to address:

• Whether PSHE ought to be statutory, either as part of the National Curriculum or through some other means of entitlement.

---

20 House of Commons Education Committee (2015). "Life lessons: PSHE and SRE in schools". https://publications.parliament.uk/pa/cm201415/cmselect/cmeduc/145/145 .pdf

- Whether the current accountability system is sufficient to ensure that schools focus on PSHE.
- The overall provision of Sex and Relationships Education in schools and the quality of its teaching, including in primary schools and academies.
- Whether recent Government steps to supplement the guidance on teaching about sex and relationships, including consent, abuse between teenagers and cyber-bullying, are adequate.
- How the effectiveness of SRE should be measured.

The inquiry took place in the wake of the House of Lords rejection of compulsory SRE earlier in that year.[21] A proposed amendment to the Children and Families Bill (that became the Children and Families Act 2014[22]) called for the introduction of compulsory relationships and sex education in state-maintained schools. However, objections included an overreliance on legislation, ineffective wording in the amendment, that it should be delivered as part of PSHE rather than its own subject area and that teaching quality might not suffice:

Baroness Eaton[23] (Con)

In the past I have met a number of parents whose children were taught PSHE in school and who found it totally inappropriate and very badly taught. I would be very concerned about how we would guarantee the quality of that kind of teaching.

And that the inclusion of anything in relation to technology would require constant updating:

Lord Nash[24] (Con)

Turning now to specific points on SRE … for children and young people to develop a good understanding of sex and relationships high-quality teaching is paramount, which is an issue that has been highlighted in this debate today. In order to teach well, teachers must have ready access to reliable and well informed sources of advice and materials. This includes recognition of the effects of digital technology, such as the potential for exposure online to inappropriate materials, to which a number of noble Lords have referred.

---

21 https://hansard.parliament.uk/Lords/2014-01-28/debates/14012881000655/Child renAndFamiliesBill#contribution-140128102000911
22 UK Government (2014). "The Children and Families Act 2014". http://www.legislati on.gov.uk/ukpga/2014/6/contents/enacted
23 https://hansard.parliament.uk/Lords/2014-01-28/debates/14012881000655/Child renAndFamiliesBill#contribution-14012889000003
24 https://hansard.parliament.uk/Lords/2014-01-28/debates/14012881000655/Child renAndFamiliesBill#contribution-14012889000034

The noble Baroness, Lady Jones, referred to the pace at which technology now moves. It is moving so quickly that it is not practical for government to keep abreast by constantly revising statutory guidance to reflect the current state of the art and the latest communications breakthroughs. For instance, Snapchat, Tumblr, Whatsapp and Chatroulette are very recent sites or apps, and any guidance that we issued would be quickly overtaken by new trends and technology that will proliferate in the future. Any revisions to guidance would soon be outflanked by the next phase of innovation.

These are common arguments against the inclusion of compulsory RSE, but miss the point that it would be possible to legislate for such a topic to be delivered by specialists if there was an appetite to do so and that a focus on technology is always flawed. While technology changes, behaviours differ little, and a focus on issues such as consent and boundaries is more fundamental to good RSE than a list of the latest apps.

Returning to the inquiry, it was interesting to note that cyberbully and sexting were both raised as aspects of personal and social development that needed to be explored within these curricula. In the summary of the report produced by the committee, they drew the following conclusion on the state of PSHE and SRE in schools:

There is a lack of clarity on the status of the subject. This must change, and we accept the argument that statutory status is needed for PSHE, with sex and relationships education as a core part of it. We recommend that the DfE develop a workplan for introducing age-appropriate PSHE and SRE as statutory subjects in primary and secondary schools, setting out its strategy for improving the supply of teachers able to deliver this subject and a timetable for achieving this. The statutory requirement should have minimal prescription content to ensure that schools have flexibility to respond to local needs and priorities. SRE should be renamed relationships and sex education to emphasise a focus on relationships.

Parental engagement is key to maximising the benefits of SRE. The Government should require schools to consult parents about the provision of SRE, and ask Ofsted to inspect the way in which schools do this. The existing right of a parent to withdraw their child from elements of SRE must be retained.

The government response to the inquiry report took some time; however, the then Secretary of State of Education did write back to the inquiry chair, Neil Carmichael MP, in January 2016.

An excerpt from that letter[25] is reproduced below, which again suggests that PSHE should be the focus for RSE, but equally, the quality of PSHE is not yet sufficiently strong to justify inclusion in the national curriculum:

---

25 Department for Education (2015). "Government Response: Life lessons: PSHE and SRE in schools". https://assets.publishing.service.gov.uk/government/uploads/system/uploads/

The vast majority of schools already make provision for PSHE and while the Government agrees that making PSHE statutory would give it equal status with other subjects, the Government is concerned that this would do little to tackle the most pressing problems with the subject, which are to do with the variable quality of its provision, as evidenced by Ofsted's finding that 40% of PSHE teaching is less than good. As such, while we will continue to keep the status of PSHE in the curriculum under review, our immediate focus will be on improving the quality of PSHE teaching in our schools.

I want PSHE to be at the heart of a whole-school ethos that is about developing the character of young people. I want it to be tailored to the individual needs of the school and for programmes to be based on the best available evidence of what works. I want senior leaders to ensure that it has the time in the curriculum and the status that it deserves within school and I want it to be taught by well-trained and well-supported staff.

Ultimately, educational responses are far more likely to provide positive outcomes than either technology or law – young people frequently comment that they never get a chance to talk about issues around sexting in their schools and certainly never get the opportunity to ask questions about it.

If one is hoping to develop a more resilient, and aware, population around image-based abuse we have to start with education in schools. Yet, how can we hope that legal protection for victims will work when they are not aware of the protection the law offers them or even that they are victims of a crime?

In 2016, the Women and Equalities Committee conducted an inquiry and published a report on sexual harassment and sexual violence in schools.[26] In that report, there was much discussion around the fact that a lot of victims of such crimes are not aware that what is happening to them is unacceptable. Many viewed such harassment, whether face to face or digital, as just a regular part of the school day. This is borne out in our own work, particularly when there is a digital element to the harassment – even with the often-repeated "don't send nudes, it's illegal" being delivered to them many times, their knowledge around the more fundamental issues such as harassment or not consenting to an image being shared by a third party is lacking and, as such, they can become victims of abuse or harassment without realising they might be protected in law, or even that the acts that they are subject to are unacceptable and potentially illegal.

Unsurprisingly, one of the main calls from this report was for compulsory RSE that was contemporary in nature (i.e. it needed to cover digital issues from a behavioural, as well as legal, perspective). However, the government response to this call

attachment_data/file/446322/Government_response_to_Life_lessons_PSHE_and_SRE_in_schools___print_version_.pdf

26 House of Commons Women's and Equalities Committee (2016). "Sexual harassment and sexual violence in schools". https://www.publications.parliament.uk/pa/cm201617/cmselect/cmwomeq/91/91.pdf

was, once again, that this was not necessary and it was down to schools to manage both RSE and the broader topic of PSHE as part of the wider school responsibility around maintaining a broad and balanced curriculum. It has been argued that such issues are now explored within the OFSTED framework,[27] and therefore, senior leaders will respond to the inspection guidance and ensure such education is in place.

Nevertheless, a report by the British Humanist Society in 2017,[28] which analysed over 2000 recent OFSTED inspections noted that PSHE, in general, is rarely addressed in these reports, and technologically related social issues are covered particularly poorly, with only 3% of reports mentioning sexting at all. It would seem, from the BHS report, that inspections do not necessarily cover all aspects of the curriculum, in particular, those that have no statutory requirement.

Eventually, the lobbying pressure seemed to result in a change of mood in the government, and in March 2017, the Department for Education and the then Secretary of State for Education, Justine Greening MP, announced[29] that they were going to develop the necessary legislation to put compulsory RSE in place, as well as launching a public consultation:

> The statutory guidance for RSE was introduced in 2000 and is becoming increasingly outdated. It fails to address risks to children which have grown in prevalence in recent years, including online pornography, sexting and staying safe online. As a result now is the right time to address these issues.
>
> The government is already taking action to address this with the introduction of a new internet safety green paper later this year, which will set out a series of steps to make the internet a safer place for young people.

This will be complemented by a comprehensive programme of engagement by the Department for Education (DfE) with stakeholders to set out suitable, age-appropriate content on RSE which focuses on mental wellbeing, consent, resilience, age-appropriate relationships and sex education, as well as keeping safe online. Regulations and statutory guidance will then be subject to full public consultation later this year, and we expect to see children and young people being taught this new curriculum in schools as soon as September 2019.

> Schools will have flexibility over how they deliver these subjects, so they can develop an integrated approach that is sensitive to the needs of the local community; and, in the case of faith schools, in accordance with their faith.

---

27 SWGfL (2017). "Making Sense of the New Online Safety Standards". *SWGfl.* http://swg fl.org.uk/news/News/online-safety/Making-Sense-of-the-New-Online-Safety-Standards
28 British Humanist Association (2017). "Happy, Safe, Healthy". *British Humanist Association.* https://humanism.org.uk/wp-content/uploads/2017-01-25-FINAL-Healthy-Ha ppy-Safe.pdf
29 Department for Education (2017). "Schools to teach 21st century relationships and sex education". https://www.gov.uk/government/news/schools-to-teach-21st-century-relat ionships-and-sex-education

We should note that even though the announcement stated September 2019, while there was a manifesto commitment to provide comprehensive relationships and sex education, the date has recently been pushed back to 2020 by the then UK Education Secretary Damien Hinds in an announcement during an Education Select Committee oral evidence session.[30]

Following consultation, the Department for Education response produced a wide-ranging response[31] that briefly mentioned online relationships and issues related to digital technology. However, there was a lack of in-depth discussion about what the digital elements for RSE might look like. Equally, the proposed modifications to the legislation brought into statute the need for schools to deliver relationships and sex education, without any specific detail on digital elements:

Amendment to the Education Act 2002

(2) In relation to education provided under section 80(1)(c) and (d), the guidance must be given with a view to ensuring that—

(a)
(b)
the pupils learn about—
(i)   the nature of marriage and its importance for family life and the bringing up of children,
(ii) safety in forming and maintaining relationships,
(iii) the characteristics of healthy relationships, and
(iv) how relationships may affect physical and mental health and well-being, and
the education is appropriate having regard to the age and the religious background of the pupils.

Section 34 Children and Social Work Act 2017

34 Education relating to relationships and sex
(1) The Secretary of State must by regulations make provision requiring—
   (a) relationships education to be provided to pupils of compulsory school age receiving primary education at schools in England;
   (b) relationships and sex education to be provided (instead of sex education) to pupils receiving secondary education at schools in England.

30 Parliament TV 2018. "Education Committee Wednesday 27 June 2018". https://www.parliamentlive.tv/Event/Index/58da6df3-da79-4b92-99cb-64a2a96d03de
31 Department for Education (2018). "Relationships education, relationships and sex education, and Health Education in England, Government consultation (including call for evidence response)". https://assets.publishing.service.gov.uk/government/uploads/system/uploads/attachment_data/file/780768/Government_Response_to_RSE_Consultation.pdf

(2) The regulations must include provision—
   (a) requiring the Secretary of State to give guidance to proprietors of schools in relation to the provision of the education and to review the guidance from time to time;
   (b) requiring proprietors of schools to have regard to the guidance;
   (c) requiring proprietors of schools to make statements of policy in relation to the education to be provided, and to make the statements available to parents or other persons;
   (d) about the circumstances in which a pupil (or a pupil below a specified age) is to be excused from receiving relationships and sex education or specified elements of that education.

(3) The regulations must provide that guidance given by virtue of subsection (2)(a) is to be given with a view to ensuring that when relationships education or relationships and sex education is given—
   (a) the pupils learn about—
      (i) safety in forming and maintaining relationships,
      (ii) the characteristics of healthy relationships, and
      (iii) how relationships may affect physical and mental health and well-being, and
   (b) the education is appropriate having regard to the age and the religious background of the pupils.

(4) The regulations may make further provision in connection with the provision of relationships education, or relationships and sex education.

On 28 March 2019, the draft statutory guidance from the Department for Education[32] was voted through by a massive majority.[33] This was then delivered as a full statutory document later in the year,[34] ready for deployment in September 2020 (the start of the new academic year in the UK). Sexting, and how schools should deal with sexting, does have implied coverage in the guidance and how schools should deal with it:

---

32 Department for Education (2019). "Relationships Education, Relationships and Sex Education (RSE) and Health Education Draft statutory guidance for Governing Bodies, Proprietors, Head Teachers, Principals, Senior Leadership Teams, Teachers. February 2019". https://assets.publishing.service.gov.uk/government/uploads/system/uploads/attachment_data/file/781150/Draft_guidance_Relationships_Education__Relationships_and_Sex_Education__RSE__and_Health_Education2.pdf
33 https://commonsvotes.digiminster.com/Divisions/Details/650
34 Department for Education (2019). "Relationships Education, Relationships and Sex Education (RSE) and Health Education Statutory guidance for Governing Bodies, Proprietors, Head Teachers, Principals, Senior Leadership Teams, Teachers". https://assets.publishing.service.gov.uk/government/uploads/system/uploads/attachment_data/file/805781/Relationships_Education__Relationships_and_Sex_Education__RSE__and_Health_Education.pdf

By the end of Primary School (Online Relationships)
   Pupils should know

- that people sometimes behave differently online, including by pretending to be someone they are not.
- that the same principles apply to online relationships as to face-to-face relationships, including the importance of respect for others online including when we are anonymous.
- the rules and principles for keeping safe online, how to recognise risks, harmful content and contact, and how to report them.
- how to critically consider their online friendships and sources of information including awareness of the risks associated with people they have never met.
- how information and data is shared and used online.

So there is some mention of concepts and behaviours related to the production and distribution of images, without explicit mentionof sexting, for example, respect for others online and recognising risk. It is encouraging to see this as these issues form the foundation of scenarios involving the exchange of indecent images, considering the roles of pressure and expectation in the sharing of images. However, at the secondary school level, some of the goals are less positive:

By the end of Secondary School (Online and media)
   Pupils should know

- their rights, responsibilities and opportunities online, including that the same expectations of behaviour apply in all contexts, including online.
- about online risks, including that any material someone provides to another has the potential to be shared online and the difficulty of removing potentially compromising material placed online.
- not to provide material to others that they would not want shared further and not to share personal material which is sent to them.
- what to do and where to get support to report material or manage issues online.

...

- that sharing and viewing indecent images of children (including those created by children) is a criminal offence which carries severe penalties including jail.

...

These goals seem to have some semblance of victim blaming about them, returning once again to tired messages such as "once it's online, it's always online", and they should not share something they would not want to have shared further. In particular, there is a strong victim blaming sentiment to "not providing materials you would not want shared further". Surely, a more progressive message would be to focus on the non-consensual sharing as the problematic behaviour? Saying never share something you wouldn't want shared further places the onus once again on the originator of the image – "well, if you hadn't shared it in the first place" is a message victims have expressed on many occasions at the Revenge Porn Helpline.

And once again the messages around legality are the driving prohibitive force around sharing images. While it is entirely valid to raise the issues about being in possession of indecent images of children, the threat of jail seems to be delivering a threatening message which is not particularly accurate for a peer on peer incident. The legal position needs to be stated, but in a progressive, non-threatening manner. The way it is defined in the draft guidance will do little to improve confidence for those victims of non-consensual sharing or image-based abuse because the focus remains victim-centric and judgemental – don't share if you don't want others to share.

However, perhaps the most concerning is the one specific mention of sexting in the entire (50 page) document:

> 82. It is important to know what the law says about sex, relationships and young people, as well as broader safeguarding issues. This includes a range of important facts and the rules regarding sharing personal information, pictures, videos and other material using technology. This will help young people to know what is right and wrong in law, but it can also provide a good foundation of knowledge for deeper discussion about all types of relationships. There are also many different legal provisions whose purpose is to protect young people and which ensure young people take responsibility for their actions. Pupils should be made aware of the relevant legal provisions when relevant topics are being taught, including for example:
>
> …
>
> • online behaviours including image and information sharing (including 'sexting', youth-produced sexual imagery, nudes, etc.)

A Youth Voice In Relationship Education

How can this be so clearly appreciated by young people yet so resolutely ignored by policymakers? Of course, discussion of legalities is important, but this should be tackled in an honest and pragmatic way. Prohibitive approaches to social education have been shown many times to not work[35,36,37] and there is no reason

---

35 South, Nigel, ed. (1988). "Drugs: Cultures, controls and Everyday Life". Sage.
36 Blackman, Shane (2010). "Youth subcultures, normalisation and drug prohibition: The politics of contemporary crisis and change?". *British Politics*, 5(3), 337–366.
37 Gilbert, Jen (2013). "Thinking in sex education: reading prohibition through the film Desire". *Sex Education*, 13(1), 30–39.

why this would be different for something like sexting. This is not what young people wish to see in the educational approaches to tackling a social issue such as image-based abuse. Yet prohibitive approaches remain the standard response by policymakers.

Throughout this book, there has been an exploration in victim perspectives around image-based abuse and many instances have been shown where blame and guilt, on the part of the victim, are fundamental responses to someone non-consensually sharing intimate images of them. There has also been much analysis of the legislation and the flaws therein. While other stakeholder responses are important (such as the need for platform providers to implement effective reporting and takedown policies that are open and transparent), we know that the most powerful driver for change will come from education. While it was encouraging to see announcements for compulsory RSE, the reality is, once again, slow progress. While it is encouraging that consent, privacy, boundaries and similar are all being covered, and schools have a statutory responsibility to deliver RSE, the guidance still fails to address the nuance around victim blaming and consent in image-based abuse.

Moreover, it should be acknowledged that while statutory guidance is one step along the path, young people state that an essential part is having knowledgeable adults they can talk to. Therefore, there is a parallel need for developments around the training of teachers and supporting resources so they can deliver the new curriculum with knowledge and confidence and answer young people's questions honestly and with conviction. However, there is certainly nothing in the statutory guidance that expects this subject to be delivered by subject specialists, and equally, the resourcing of the roll-out results in cause for concern. The Department for Education has committed £6 million to this deployment. In total, across England and Wales, there are 25,898 schools,[38] so with a crude calculation that amounts to approximately £232 per school. This does not seem like sufficient funding for effective staff training or a dedicated post.

This chapter has explored both the need for education, as underpinned by empirical evidence, and also the current state of legislation and statutory guidance within the UK. In order for a societal change in attitudes towards image-based abuse and the non-consensual sharing of images, there is a need for a sound, effective educational base in order to tackle this. While it is acknowledged that public education programmes are difficult, particularly when attempting to communicate about complex issues, there is an opportunity to build an attitude change into primary and secondary education with young people. However, the evidence presented so far regarding what this education might look like does not give much enthusiasm for a shift in attitude or a move from victim blaming. While there are steps in the right direction (such as teaching consent in primary schools), the fact that the only formal mention of sexting in the draft guidance

38 https://www.besa.org.uk/key-uk-education-statistics/

relates to legalities highlights that this guidance (and the lack of resourcing for delivering in schools) is hardly likely to cause a paradigm shift.

Therefore, what is likely to happen without effective RSE? Through work with young people and also with the Revenge Porn Helpline, there seems to be a tolerance of image-based abuse in society – victims will be blamed, the standard responses of "well, if you hadn't taken the image they wouldn't have been able to share it" emerges, from both stakeholders and bystanders, and victims feel either responsible or, worse, revictimised by the responses of others. We have seen little change in attitudes in schools in ten years, and that should be no surprise given the nature of education in the UK around image-based abuse, and it seems little is going to change. Therefore, tolerance is likely to increase and victims to remain unsupported.

One thing of which all stakeholder should be mindful when considering legislation affecting young people is the UN Convention on the Rights of the Child.[39] More specifically, in this case, Article 29, which relates to the Goals of Education:

Article 29 (goals of education)
1. States Parties agree that the education of the child shall be directed to:
   (a) The development of the child's personality, talents and mental and physical abilities to their fullest potential;
   (b) The development of respect for human rights and fundamental freedoms, and for the principles enshrined in the Charter of the United Nations;
   (c) The development of respect for the child's parents, his or her own cultural identity, language and values, for the national values of the country in which the child is living, the country from which he or she may originate, and for civilizations different from his or her own;
   (d) The preparation of the child for responsible life in a free society, in the spirit of understanding, peace, tolerance, equality of sexes, and friendship among all peoples, ethnic, national and religious groups and persons of indigenous origin;
   (e) The development of respect for the natural environment.

Indeed, in 2010, the government produced a "work in progress" which aimed to show how legislation underpins the UN CRC in the UK,[40] and claimed that (paragraph 7.46):

39 United Nations (1989). "UN Convention of the Rights of the Child". https://downloads.unicef.org.uk/wp-content/uploads/2010/05/UNCRC_united_nations_convention_on_the_rights_of_the_child.pdf?_ga=2.199875755.401103239.1553966569-432177925.1552825742
40 Department for Education (2010). "The United Nations Convention on the Rights of the Child: How legislation underpins implementation in England". https://assets.publishing

for personal, social, health and economic education (PSHE) to be compulsory for pupils aged 11 to 16, and for understanding physical development, health and wellbeing to be compulsory for pupils aged five to 11. PSHE will include, amongst other things, education about emotional health and wellbeing, sex and relationships education, careers, business and economic education.

However, the current legislation around education related to image-based abuse is still very much failing young people in their rights around goals of education. Parts (b) and (d) in particular seem not to be addressed effectively within current legislation, and as a result, we are also impacting on other rights such as

- **Article 12** (respect for the views of the child)
- **Article 16** (right to privacy)
- **Article 19** (protection from violence, abuse and neglect)
- **Article 34** (sexual exploitation)

Without effective education around image-based abuse, children and young people are placed at risk of sexual exploitation and abuse. A solution that ensures they are "prohibited" from sending an indecent image would impact significantly on their privacy and is clearly failing to respect the views of the child because, as we have highlighted in this book, young people have called for a long time for the same things from stakeholders in their safeguarding – they should be informed, they should listen and they should not judge. Yet, instead, there is the development of policy after policy that tells them "don't do this, because if you do, you're breaking the law".

In bringing this chapter to a close, this has been somewhat critical of the current education provision around image-based abuse in UK schools, and considerations of the emerging new statutory curriculum give little enthusiasm that things will improve in the near future. The potential impact on society that this dearth of education might have can be learned from the past – adult victims of image-based abuse blame themselves and consider themselves deserving of abuse for sharing images consensually with someone they trusted. It is worthwhile, therefore, to explore how things might improve. Young people want support and knowledgeable adults they can turn to. The act of image exchange is rarely the problem, abuse arises from the non-consensual sharing of the image and subsequent abuse. There is a need to move away from education that focuses on the act, the ever-changing and adapting nature of the production and distribution of self-generated explicit images among both teen and adult populations means that policy will always be trying to catch up. There is a need to get away from the act and instead focus on the harm to the victim and impact, and that just because

---

.service.gov.uk/government/uploads/system/uploads/attachment_data/file/296368/un crc_how_legislation_underpins_implementation_in_england_march_2010.pdf

you have shared an image, it does not mean you have to accept any abuse that arises as a result.

If the law is to be used within this context, it needs to be used properly. Rather than focusing, once again, on the production and distribution of the image in the first instance, talk about the legislative dimensions that arise from abuse, and call them for what they are – sexual abuse, harassment, blackmail, coercion and so on. Online versus offline differentiation is not useful, given the behaviours are the same regardless of the originating act. It gives an unnecessary distinction and makes it easy for legislators and policymakers to make out it is different. Sexting is not an "online" crime, and neither is the abuse that arises from it. While technology facilitates both the distribution and the abuse, there is nothing about the online element that makes the abuse different.

Adults with the responsibility for children's safeguarding and education should hopefully allow them to develop into resilient adults who will equally be aware of their rights related to the non-consensual sharing of intimate images and how unacceptable the resultant abuse they might be subjected to is. We, as adult stakeholders in this space, need to stop thinking we know best when it comes to education. Prejudiced and biased views on what "works" with education should not be imposed on young people, or look to assuage the more vocal, yet potentially less numerous, voices that suggest educating young people about healthy relationships somehow encourages them to engage in deviant behaviour.[41,42] Most importantly, there is a need to stop thinking as adults and instead involve the youth voice in the development of policy that affects them. There is now a wealth of research that discusses these issues, yet the broader context that young people are calling for is still not being addressed. If we hope to move societal thinking and the response to image-based abuse forwards, we have to address it in compulsory education. This is not a cultural shift that will happen without policy change, and in this book, there are many examples of victims being treated appallingly by both society and also those supposedly responsible for their safeguarding. Progressive approaches need to be adopted, children and young people are calling for this, there is a need for this education to be delivered by experts, not just people who have a light workload or an enthusiasm for social media. Perhaps the most enlightened legislation would be to introduce this as statute, rather than prohibitive laws that punish or fail to protect victims, or legislation that hints at progression then draws back when the political winds change.

41 Magra, I. (2019). "England Greatly Expands Sex Education, Despite Some Parents' Protests". *The New York Times.* https://www.nytimes.com/2019/02/26/world/europe/sex-education-uk.html

42 UK Government and Parliamentary Petitions (2019). "Give parents the right to opt their child out of Relationship and Sex Education". https://petition.parliament.uk/petitions/235053

8 Conclusion

The focus of this text relates to UK legislation, as this is the jurisdiction in which this research has taken place. However, image-based abuse is not a UK specific issue and these social and legislative challenges are widespread and relevant to legal scholars and practitioners outside of the UK. Moreover, this is not merely an exploration of the UK legislation and policy space around image-based abuse. It is a case study on how the criminal justice system and wider safeguarding stakeholder groups tackle emerging and challenging sociotechnical issues and how they can get it wrong. There is nothing specific to the UK regarding the non-consensual sharing of intimate images, this is an issue faced by all nations in their attempts to protect their citizens from harm and punish those who do not wish to align with the socially agreed rules of society.

Overreliance on a single stakeholder in this space is doomed to fail and the well-trodden path by politicians of laying responsibility at the door of service providers, to make claims that they are responsible for such problems and therefore should "do more" to prevent them, fails to understand the root cause of behaviours and the social context in which they exist. There are many examples of this, both within the context of revenge pornography and sexting and beyond it (for example, pornography, cyberbullying and radicalisation). The Politician's Fallacy is writ large over this area – there is widespread social concern, so they have to do "something". However, that "something" is not always well thought out, or, as is the case related to image-based abuse, more of an exercise in deflection than a mature response.

With image-based abuse, there is only so much a service provider can do. With concepts like indecency difficult to define even for human intervention, particularly around "thresholds" for what constitutes legality, one can see an even greater challenge for a technological intervention. While technology is extremely good at literal matching at a data level (i.e. keywords, image data, filenames), interpretation is far more challenging, and algorithms are simply not capable of making those judgements beyond training sets. The algorithms operate in such a way that a human interpretation of what is actually happening may not be the reality of the underlying functionality.

Moreover, the flaws in such technologically mediated interventions can result in serious compromises in the rights of victims. While the criminal justice response to the challenge of image-based abuse is improving (mainly in the case of adult victims), both in terms of the protection of victims and the pragmatism exercised in the interpretation of the relevant law in sexting cases, it still does not provide an effective or complete solution. Whether solutions actually exist in this context is a deeply philosophical question. Can one achieve a social state when no one will take an intimate (however this is defined) image of themselves and send it? The prevalent message for many years related to teen sexting is "they should not be doing it". The question posted by education and social care professionals, policymakers and politicians has not changed in over ten years – "how can we stop children sexting?". The simple answer is that we cannot. While legislation is starting to help victims post-age of majority, there seems little evidence to show the practice is slowing down among the adult population and the confused, draconian approach to "policing" teen sexting, alongside a punitive educational approach, has done nothing to prevent this practice being carried out by minors. While we would very much like it to be the case that no minor would engage in the exchange of intimate image, it is a very naïve starting point for policy and law to assume this could be the case.

It would seem to be quite a dystopian vision to consider a state where, through technological monitoring and heuristics, coupled with strongly implemented legislation, a human choice to engage in such practices was eliminated. Therefore, perhaps we should avoid using the term "solution" to address these issues and explore in more detail how education might empower those who may potentially be engaging in the exchange of intimate image practices and protect them if the images are non-consensually shared further. If victims are aware that the resultant abuse that arises as a result of the distribution of an image (without their consent), at least they have some way of addressing the abuse, rather than the view often communicated to us by both adult and minor victims:

I shouldn't have taken the picture in the first place.

Governments' role as stakeholders needs exploring with more in-depth detail too – there are clear calls from both young people and adult victims of image-based abuse for policymakers to "do more" around education. Public health and education policy that focuses upon prevention through prohibition is problematic and a perspective that considers risk management and resilience could do more to positively impact on supporting those who become victims of abuse as a result of sharing images. Prohibitive approaches are not working, and a more progressive solution is needed, both legally and educationally, rather than hoping that one can prohibit the problem through technological intervention and private sector censorship. If offenders are more aware of the potential legal ramifications of their actions, they may be dissuaded from such acts. If victims have knowledge of the fact that they have been subject to illegal abuse, rather than turning educative messages upon themselves, perhaps they would be in a more resilient place to tackle the harm. Yet, in general, the government still to tries to avoid engaging with educational interventions with this problem, as can be seen from the examination of the RSE curriculum, soon to be implemented RSE curriculum in England.

In drawing this book to a close, there are a number of recommendations that are proposed as a result of the legislative and empirical analysis. While there is some positive progress within the legislation with s33 of the Criminal Justice and Courts Act, in that it made the act of non-consensually sharing an intimate in order to cause harm illegal, there is still much that might be done to improve the plight of victims. From the perspective of adult image-based abuse, we would recommend the following.

The reclassification of image-based abuse as a sexual, rather than communications, crime, as this would provide victims with a level on anonymity in the reporting of offences, and therefore, it is more likely they would come forward to report abuse. Moreover, the view of image-based abuse as a communication crime, purely because the mode of abuse utilises digital communications technology, allows a societal reaction that looks at the abuse as something done online, rather than recognising it more accurately as a form of domestic abuse that might be being used in conjunction with other forms of abuse.

The introduction of the threat to share as an offence in the England and Wales legislation. While this is already in place in the Scottish legislation, it does not exist for victims in England and Wales. As we have discussed throughout this text, there is much power in the threat to share intimate images. In some way, there is more power because, once images have been shared, the abuser has less coercive power over the victim. The addition of threat to the legislation would also bring parity with Scottish legislation.

Finally, with legislation that focuses on forms of image-based abuse, intent remains problematic. If the legislation states that intent to distress or cause harm is required for the crime to have been committed, there is a straightforward defence for the abuser, and a challenge for the prosecution to prove this intent. Surely, the impact on the victim should be given greater credence? While the abuser might claim they have shared an image as a joke, if the impact of the victim is severe, should that be a reasonable defence?

For legislation related to teen sexting, there is no easy answer. This is no longer legislation that can be fixed with policy sticking plasters – the application of outcome 21 recording overcame the requirement to establish a criminal record for a minor who has disclosed intimate images of themselves to someone else, but it does not absolve them from liability should a future record check result in a chief constable deciding the sharing of said images should be disclosed. As a result of the exploration of Hansard and case law, it is simply being applied to acts for which it was not intended to be used. When a "21st-century" behaviour of the consensual sharing of an intimate image by a minor is used to prosecute or threaten to charge a victim of the further non-consensual sharing of said image, using legislation intended to protect children from abuse by adults, we are failing victims. Moreover, victims are experiencing revictimising when they are already vulnerable and being subject to abuse by isolating them and making them feel that they cannot ask for help due to the threat of arrest. The sort of victim impacts explored among the adult population as a result of the non-consensual sharing of intimate images do not begin at 18, minors are also subject to the same impacts. There is a need for new legislation that protects the victim, whatever their age, and focuses instead on the non-consensual sharing of intimate images.

This is not to say this legislation should give carte blanche to minors to engage in the exchange of intimate images, this is still a problematic behaviour, but punitive threats are not effective, and the law at present can result in further harm to the victim. An education curriculum that approaches the exchange of intimate images, and associated image-based abuse, in a progressive manner that allows for the discussion of fundamental relationship education topics such as consent, respect and boundaries is likely to be more effective, and it is certainly something minors call for themselves. A refocus on education around the fact that the non-consensual sharing of images is wrong, alongside effective legislation that can be applied when such acts are carried out, should shift cultural blame from the victim to the sharer. Allowing these behaviours in minors can embolden attitudes that are carried into adult life. Young people we have spoken to recognise the use of threat to share as a coercive measure, but equally do not see anything wrong with it. Is it any wonder, therefore, that, unchallenged, they will take these attitudes into adulthood?

And finally, the delivery of this education also needs addressing. This is not a subject that can be delivered by anyone, and relationships and sex education should be recognised as a subject of equal importance to academic subjects, delivered by those who both understand the issues and can also deliver education in an inclusive, informed manner. Whether this is something where legislation might play a part is debatable, however, established scrutiny mechanisms could be reinforced to make this part of the expected framework for inspection in schools and colleges.

This text has conducted a detailed exploration of image-based abuse, the experiences of those who have been abused and the legislation that can support it, or, in some cases, revictimise victims. The impact on victims of all ages can be severe. This is not an issue that will disappear, as discussed above, we will not reach a time when citizens no longer choose to take and send intimate images – the technology exists for this in a way it was not even 20 years ago, and this will not change. Neither should we expect citizens to stop engaging in such practices – freedom of expression is a fundamental right, and there is no reason why people should be prevented from doing so. However, as a society, our obsession with the act, rather than the non-consensual sharing, means that, often, victims are left harmed and vulnerable to further abuse as a result of the actions of abusers. While the law has come some way to protect victims, there is still a long way to go.

Index

For Product Safety Concerns and Information please contact our EU
representative GPSR@taylorandfrancis.com
Taylor & Francis Verlag GmbH, Kaufingerstraße 24, 80331 München, Germany